IN SPITE OF…

TREOPIA GREEN WASHINGTON

To my family

CONTENTS

INTRODUCTION

Even though my mother was adamant about not talking about yourself, I have been persuaded that, "You are not talking about yourself, you are telling things people need to hear." The result is this book: *In Spite Of....*

This book describes my life experiences and events, beginning in Little Rock, Arkansas (my birthplace), when "Jim Crow" and segregation laws were alive and well. Of greater importance, however, are the successes achieved—in spite of.

Our parents reared us to have confidence and to know that we could accomplish many things in our lives. This philosophy undoubtedly helped my brother through one of the most difficult years of his life—to integrate Little Rock Central High School, as the only senior of the Little Rock Nine. He chose to become one of the "Nine," not because he was trying to "make history," but because he was a sixteen-year-old from a family who knew that he deserved the best education possible and was as capable as anyone to pursue it. He accomplished what many had hoped he would not—and many actively tried to prevent him from doing so—he graduated.

My brother's story was followed in the news. Many were inspired by his commitment and perseverance, and some made decisions that changed the course of history. The North Carolina lunch counter sit-in students, and Congressman John Lewis, both talked about being inspired by Ernest's courage. Others followed his story and were forever changed. They saw a boy, a student, like themselves, a young person their age, with whom they had more in common than they had been taught to believe. A person who believed in his ability and wanted to get a good education, a young person who had dreams and ambition for his life.

The same can be said of my mother and aunt, who many years earlier, joined a small group of Dunbar High School teachers to sue the Little Rock School Board for equal pay for Black teachers. They firmly believed in this mission, and they won, with the help of the NAACP attorney, Thurgood Marshall.

The course of action demonstrated by my family, has provided me with the courage and ability to enjoy fourteen wonderful career experiences; each of which resulted from the preceding career. We were taught to "Always do your best, whatever the task, because you never know what the next step will be." In addition, we were taught to "Follow your mind, and do what is right." These teachings were also a factor in my decision to confront the University of Arkansas, to rectify their denial of my mother's participation in commencement activities, after she had successfully completed all requirements for her master's degree in 1951.

The experiences and events described in this book, are the result of our family's philosophies for living. Our family instilled in us the belief that there are choices, daily choices: the decision to stick to a commitment; the decision to do your homework, to study, to get an education; and most of all, to take full responsibility for your actions. These decisions made the difference.

My hope is that this information might inspire others to try it too…In spite of.

ONE

LITTLE ROCK

On Monday September 2, 1957, as I was teaching my class of thirty-two Baltimore kindergarteners, I was surprised to see my principal at my classroom door. I will never forget the urgency in her voice as she said, "Treopia! Did you hear about the rioting in Little Rock?" Her words stunned me. My response conveyed my disbelief. "What?" I said. "People there don't riot."

In late August my brother Ernest and eight other African American students had been getting ready to begin their school year at Little Rock Central High School. I had graduated from college two years earlier, and my younger brother, Scott, was still in junior high school. Ernest and the others would be the first students to desegregate Central, one of the first high schools in America to be desegregated after the 1954 Supreme Court ruling in *Brown v. Board of Education*, which found that racial segregation in public schools violated the Fourteenth Amendment of the Constitution. The students came to be known as the "Little Rock Nine."

I was at home, in Little Rock, that August visiting my family before returning to my second year of teaching kindergarten in Baltimore. When I said goodbye to my family on Sunday and flew back to Baltimore, I could never have imagined what would unfold

3

in the days ahead. Ernest would be starting his senior year of high school. We expected some people to be upset about the turn of events. However, my family and my community assumed that after "the kinks were worked out" things would eventually settle down.

I could not believe people would riot in Little Rock because I had experienced a safe and nurturing community there growing up. However, that safety existed within the narrow confines of the Black community and the security my parents created for me and my brothers at home. My parents and the adults in my community protected us fiercely, and as I matured, I came to understand how tenuous and hard-fought my comfort was, growing up in the completely segregated world of the Jim Crow South. Jim Crow laws were enacted in the South after the Civil War, and they mandated racial segregation in public spaces. "Jim Crow" was a character in minstrel shows in the 1800s, and the term "Jim Crow" was used as a derogatory way to refer to a Black man. These laws governed daily life in the Southern states for nearly one hundred years until the Civil Rights Act in the 1960s overturned that legislation.

The rules surrounding race during that time were very rigid. Black people, referred to as Negroes or colored people, were not allowed in restaurants or hotels in the South. We were not permitted to sit at lunch counters in stores. If we took the bus, we had to sit in the back. If we went to the movie theater, we had to sit in the balcony. We could go to the public zoo (Fair Park in Little Rock), but we were not permitted to use the public swimming pool. We could not stay in hotels when traveling or rent them for functions, such as wedding parties or club meetings. The only way people of color could enter hotels, in most southern cities, was to work in the hotel.

It's difficult for someone who did not experience it to imagine, but everything in my childhood world was segregated. Neighborhoods were segregated. Churches were segregated. My elementary school, my junior high, and high school were segregated. Everything was completely segregated until my brother, Ernest, and eight other students entered Central High School in the fall of 1957.

***

I grew up on 21st and Pulaski Streets in a close-knit Black neighborhood. Many of my neighbors were teachers, small business owners, nurses, and lawyers. I lived with my parents and two younger brothers just four blocks from the Black high school, Dunbar, where my aunt and mother were teachers.

The extended neighborhood had a number of Black-owned small businesses (but in downtown Little Rock there were no Black clerks in stores). On the next corner from where we lived there was Powell's Grocery Store. One of our neighbors owned a funeral home, and there was a florist shop about seven blocks from our house. I went to kindergarten with the florist's son. That year, my mother planned a Valentine's Day party for me. One of the guests was the florist's son, who brought me a red and white carnation wrist corsage. My first flowers!

Our neighbor, Mrs. Shropshire, was an elementary school teacher. She and her husband, who worked on the railroad, had three sons who were also high-achieving Dunbar High School graduates. One went on to become vice president of Miller Brewing Company, another became the first Black judge in Gary, Indiana, and the third became a dentist in Atlanta. I remember riding with Mrs. Shropshire to nursery school at Stephens Elementary school, where she taught.

Next door lived a family whose son was my classmate at Dunbar. He later became dean of Arts and Sciences at Southern University in Baton Rouge, and his sister was a principal at a school in St. Louis. Another neighbor had a son who was a journalist for the *Washington Post* and later was the *Post's* foreign bureau chief. Following his sudden passing overseas, the *Post* held a luncheon for his mother, which I was privileged to attend. Another neighbor around the corner, who also graduated from Dunbar, became the first Black millionaire salesman for Allstate Insurance.

I list these successes not to brag about my neighbors growing up, but to give a sense of the environment we were raised in. We were encouraged to go places and do things. During that era, it was assumed we would go away to college and move North or West to seek opportunities away from the Jim Crow laws that existed in the South. These laws constrained not only daily life, but also ambition, dreams, and economic expansion for Negroes (as we were known then).

When we were encouraged by the community to go elsewhere to seek our fortunes, we weren't being pushed out; we were being encouraged to go out, and there's a big difference. In many ways we were insulated in our neighborhood and church communities. The adults there supported us and had great expectations for what we would become.

Although the Jim Crow laws of the time prohibited us from doing many things, my parents provided experiences that enabled us to grow up without feeling deprived. Every summer I went North with my cousin or my aunt to visit St. Louis or Chicago, where Jim Crow laws did not exist. Later I realized that this was my parents' way of giving me experiences, like eating in restaurants or going to the theater, where I could sit anywhere I wished. My parents never articulated this, however; we just did things.

6

They were skillful at navigating a system designed to "put them in their place." Their attitude was, "This may be the way things are, but this is what we are going to do."

My mother used to say to me, "You're going to meet people of all races, and in every situation, there are going to be people you like more than others and people who seem better to you than others, and that has nothing to do with race." My mother's wisdom has stayed with me throughout my life, and I have been enriched by meeting people whose life experiences and races were different from mine.

In spite of everything my parents must have experienced in their lives I never heard the word "hate" used in our house. Never. Even when Ernest was going through the '57 Crisis at Little Rock Central High School.

TWO

FAMILY

My mother, Lothaire Scott Green, was a very dignified person, not pretentiously dignified, but she carried an aura of dignity about her. My mother's moral strength must have come from her parents. My maternal grandmother passed when I was three, so I never really knew her, but I was very close with my grandfather. I did not know my paternal grandparents since they passed before I was born.

I have wondered if my great-grandparents were born into slavery, but I did not hear any stories about my ancestors growing up. My parents and grandparents did not talk much about our family history, and we didn't ask. There are things we don't know because they were just not in the conversation. It's like a locked box of stories in time. I remember overhearing one story, however, and it was about my grandfather when he tried to vote in the early 1900s. He was run off with a shotgun. Literally run off with a shotgun for trying to vote.

I think people didn't talk about the past because many things were so horrid at that time. For instance, I didn't know until recently about the 1921 Greenwood Massacre in Tulsa, when thirty blocks of an area known as "Black Wall Street" were burned to the ground, and it's estimated more than one hundred Black people were killed. When I was in high school the biggest football game of the year was against Tulsa, and we never heard about the massacre that had happened only 25 years earlier. It was never mentioned.

There was also a riot in Arkansas, the Elaine Massacre of 1919, where hundreds of Black people were killed by a White mob. I recently talked with our family friend, a retired educator, Lucille McCall, and she remembered hearing of the massacre. Growing up I never knew anything about it, although it happened in Phillips County, the same county as my father's hometown. I would like to have known more about my ancestors, but people didn't talk about those things; their focus was on now and the future.

I think about the courage of adults back in that day. My parents just didn't talk about what they couldn't do. They only talked about what they aspired to do. That was the kind of encouragement we received. They didn't want us to carry this heavy burden of the racism in society, as children. They wanted us to focus on what children can do: play nicely, do well in school, be the best person you can be. Don't worry about anything else. They protected our innocence in childhood to the best of their ability.

***

My grandfather, Eugene Scott, was born in 1873 in South Carolina and later moved to Little Rock. He was a postman. When he carried the mail, he was known to wear a three-piece suit, not a uniform. That was his choice. He was a gentleman and very proper. It was important to be proper in those days, especially in the South.

My grandfather was self-taught because there were very few schools for Black children when he was growing up. He was an avid reader, particularly of Greek mythology. He gave his daughters, my mother and her sister, the unusual names "Lothaire" and "Treopia." The story goes that he felt his own name, "Eugene," was far too common and he did not want his children to have common names.

My mother and aunt were raised in the city of Little Rock and accustomed to the sounds of a busy city. My mother told me a story of going with her sister to visit friends in the country and crying all night because she was scared—it was too quiet!

When my mother and aunt were growing up in the early 1900s, they did all the proper things that young Black girls at the time could do. Arts, culture, and learning were valued in my grandparents' household. My mother took music lessons and played the violin.

My mother was a bit more reserved in personality compared to my aunt. My aunt was the more assertive one. She was two years older than my mother. I was born five minutes after my aunt's birthday, so I was known as "Little Treopia," and my aunt was "Big Treopia."

My maiden name was "Treopia Clara Green." "Treopia" after my mother's sister and "Clara" after one of my father's sisters. My mother was the most equitable person in the world, so she made sure my father's family was represented as well when naming me.

Growing up I resented the uniqueness of my name. I could never find any trinket with my name monogrammed on it. But as I matured, I appreciated the uniqueness. If you ever run into another "Treopia" I can guarantee her roots are in Arkansas. More than a few of my aunt's former students named their daughters after her.

My mother and aunt both attended the historically Black college, Wilberforce, in Ohio, to become teachers. It was a big deal in those days to go away that far to college. The fact that it was in a northern state meant they would not be subjected to the restrictions of Jim Crow laws like they were at home in Little Rock. It was also necessary to matriculate at an HBCU (historically Black college or university) because Black students could not attend White colleges in the South.

My mother majored in home economics in order to become a teacher and she played on the women's basketball team. She graduated in 1924, earning her two-year degree. My mother and aunt later went to Arkansas AM&N in Pine Bluff (now the University of Arkansas at Pine Bluff) and completed their four-year degrees in 1934.

A talented seamstress, my mother apprenticed for a year with a tailor and another year with a milliner while in college. Her tailoring was impeccable. My mother taught me to sew, and I mastered the rudiments. Her standard was perfection, and if it wasn't done right, you had to rip it up and start all over again. I ripped up more things than I started! She had a talent for sewing that I did not have. I knew as I became older that I was not going to be like her in that way.

For Black college-educated women the early choices for careers were limited to teacher, nurse, or sometimes social worker. Dreams of having other careers often died quickly because that was simply not allowed. It wasn't that ambitions were squashed per se, it was that you didn't even think about doing other things.

For instance, I enjoyed taking ballet lessons as a girl and had aspirations for a couple seconds of becoming a ballerina, but I never thought about it seriously because it seemed impossible. I thought, "I couldn't pursue that," and very quicky it was just out of the question in my mind as a future career.

Like my grandfather, my uncle, Lytle Gravelly, Aunt Treopia's husband, was also a postman, and her son-in-law was one as well. Being a postal carrier was one of the best occupations available at that time for African American men. My uncle went to college, but there were very few career opportunities for educated Black men. Also, Black postal carriers were not in supervisory positions in the postal service, so they did not benefit from having connections or the help of a business network either.

This was Jim Crow. There were limits placed on people of color that prevented them from rising up through the ranks to become managers. My aunt's son-in-law eventually became a post office branch manager after the civil rights laws were enacted in the 1960s.

***

My father, Ernest Green, was a World War I veteran and was stationed at one point, in Marseilles, France. I remember the first words he taught me to say were, "Parlez-vous français?" I have always had a love for the French language because of that and took French in high school. Like most African American soldiers in World War I, he was not on the front lines and was probably in a role of servitude in the army, but he never discussed that with me.

My father was not one to complain about anything, and he worked incredibly hard. He was not a highly educated man academically but supported everything my mother did and valued our education. I doubt my father got past elementary school, which was common at that time.

I don't know how my parents met. Daddy was from Helena, Arkansas, a port town on the Mississippi River. He settled in Little Rock after returning from service in World War I. After Mother's graduation from Wilberforce, she was offered a scholarship to the Pratt Institute of Design in New York because of her talent in dressmaking, but she declined in favor of returning to Little Rock, and they were married the next year in 1925.

My father was born on July 25, 1888, and my mother was born on March 6, 1899, so there was an eleven-year age difference between them. He and my mother were married for eleven years before I was born, so they were older parents and more mature. I think that made a big difference in how we were brought up. They had a lot of wisdom by the time they raised us.

Daddy worked as a custodian at the U.S. Post Office in Little Rock. He worked in the post office during the day and most evenings during the week and weekend he served dinners with a caterer, or he worked at the Little Rock Country Club, serving wealthy people. The postmistress, Mrs. Robinson, was the wife of Senator Robinson, and when prominent people came to town, Mrs. Robinson often hosted dinners at her home, and my father served those dinners.

My mother said that when she was carrying me, President Franklin D. Roosevelt came to town and Daddy served the party and had her come over so she could see President Roosevelt. I was born about one month after that.

One time Daddy served a party for a big wedding. He knew we liked pretty things, so he called and told Mother to bring me to the house while the family was at the church, so I could see the gorgeous decorations. In those days servitude was the occupation that a great majority of people of color had. I'm sure my father endured racism, but he didn't talk about it with me.

I never knew much about my father's family, because they had all moved away when I was very young, or even before I was born. I realize now how much I missed not knowing about them. My father had three sisters, and they all did some kind of service for wealthy people. One moved to Washington, DC because she served dinners for one of the congressmen.

Later, as part of the Great Migration when millions of Black people left the South in search of better jobs, his other two sisters moved out to Oakland, California. One year, on my eighth birthday, one of my aunts in California sent me a crystal vase etched in gold. I wish I had it now, but as an eight-year-old I was almost insulted to receive this beautiful thing. I remember thinking, "What am I going to do with this?"

My father worked many long hours to provide for our family. He made sure that in our home, we had the same kinds of things and lived in the same sort of style as the homes in which he served. On Sundays every week we would have dinner in the dining room with a linen tablecloth, linen napkins, and china. We learned proper table etiquette from my mother. My younger brother Scott used to say we grew up by Emily Post, the etiquette guru. One of the things instilled in me from my earliest years was to always "act like a lady."

Often, Daddy would bring home leftovers from the dinners he served, so we would have filet mignon almost every week. I didn't realize until I had to buy it myself how uncommon this was. He would also bring home petit fours and all kinds of fancy dishes. My brothers didn't like the fancy food and preferred to eat baloney sandwiches or peanut butter and jelly.

Once Daddy brought a lobster home and when I opened the refrigerator this huge lobster scared the daylights out of me!

During hunting season, he would bring home pheasant and would tell us, "Watch out for the buckshot."

When Daddy didn't have a party to serve, he would help Mother cook dinner. My parents' marriage was a partnership. I thought every family worked that way, until I grew older and realized, unfortunately, this was not the case.

My mother was a wonderful cook and enjoyed creating her own fancy dishes, but she was also a health proponent before that kind of thing was popular. She had us take cod liver oil every morning and eat vegetables every day. Nothing was fried and there was a green vegetable at every meal. "Soul food" was not on the menu! None of us grew up to have any major health problems, and I credit my mother's health regimen for that.

The rule in our house was, you eat what has been prepared for you. Period. One time we were at my parents' friends' house for dinner when I was very young. The lady turned to me and said, "Treopia, what would you like?" And my mother immediately said, "You don't ask her what she wants. She eats what you prepare." That was the way we grew up.

I remember Mother loved to prepare steamed okra in the summer. My youngest brother Scott hated okra. One day I remember she went to the kitchen and while she was gone Scott put the okra in his pocket. When she came back, she said, "Oh, I see you finished all the okra." I didn't say anything! My brothers were much more daring than I ever would have been.

In the summer a White farmer we called "the vegetable man" would park his blue pickup truck on the street in our neighborhood and sell produce from his truck. My mother always bought fresh corn or whatever vegetables he was selling that day. We had several fig trees in our backyard and every summer Mother enjoyed preserving the figs. She also canned peaches in the summer to keep for the winter. How she found the time to do all that, I will never know. She was always busy, but not rushed, just always doing something productive.

My mother and father lived strictly by the Golden Rule: "Do unto others as you would have them do unto you." Growing up, it was reinforced for me and my brothers, Ernest and Scott, that with whatever we did, our parents' attitude was, "Remember, you can always do better." They believed it's what you do, and how you treat others, that matters, not who you are.

My father reinforced whatever my mother suggested. There was not a lot of preaching, like "Do this" or "You have to be this." It was demonstrated. It was who they really were. Even now, though my mother has been gone since 1976, sometimes I'll do something and think "Would my mother approve of this?"

I marvel at my mother's strength and inner conviction. She was a very modest and unassuming person. She didn't seek attention for herself, but people in our community not only respected her, they also looked to her for leadership. They called her for help with wedding planning or advice about how to handle a problem with a child. She was always willing to help and do what she could, but never to the extent that she neglected us at home.

My mother's philosophies have guided me throughout my life and strengthened me through the years. She always supported us. We grew up with the notion that the things we did were totally supported, and it was always expected that we would do the right thing.

We knew she and my father expected us to do well, but they never told us things like, "You are so beautiful," or "You are so smart." My mother would always say, "Beauty is inner, it's how a person behaves that makes them beautiful." I remember once my mother's friend said to me when I was very young, "Oh, aren't you so cute!" And to that my mother said, "The only things that are cute are monkeys and babies."

Another of my mother's philosophies that has served me well through the years: if you have an issue, you analyze it, determine what you can do about it, do what you can, and then leave it alone. She believed that there should be no such thing as "worry." She used to say, "There is nothing that should interfere with a good night's sleep because there's nothing much you can do about anything between 11:00 at night and 7:00 the next morning. So, you might as well just go to sleep and get up the next day and deal with whatever you have to deal with."

In my life I really try to practice those things, sometimes subconsciously, sometimes consciously, and it works.

Mother: Lothaire Scott Green

Daddy: Ernest Gideon Green

(L-R) Ernest (3 years old), Scott (1 year old), Treopia Green (8 years old). Mother made my green and white checked dress.

(L-R) Scott, Ernest, and Treopia. Standing at the entrance of our home in Little Rock. It was placed on the National Register of Historic Places.

My brothers and I in our front yard. Our neighbors' house is visible across the street. Mr. Jackson was a brick mason and built their home.

Our house on 21st and Pulaski in Little Rock. The porch is where Mother and I would sew in the summer.

THREE

CHILDHOOD

As a little girl, I had a baby doll and a "grown-up" doll. My baby doll was named "Bertha," I think for one of my mother's close friends. When I was about three, I told my mother one day that it was Bertha's birthday. My mother said I should take my baby doll for a walk, so I put Bertha in her wicker buggy and walked up the sidewalk to a couple of neighbors' houses. When I came back home, my mother had baked a birthday cake and put one candle in it, and we had a birthday party for Bertha.

My other doll was a larger "Judy Garland doll." Mother made all of my clothes growing up and would sometime make matching outfits for my doll. She once made a burgundy wool, velvet collar coat for me, and she made an identical one for my doll. Sewing was her hobby, a kind of respite from long hours of teaching. My Judy Garland doll was extremely well dressed!

Birthdays were always celebrated in our home. My mother enjoyed cooking and doing fancy luncheons. My birthday, July 3, was just one day after my Aunt Treopia's birthday on July 2. We would always celebrate our birthdays together, and the next day, celebrate the Fourth of July. Every year my mother made me a red, white, and blue outfit to wear for the Fourth celebration.

My nursery school was at Stephens Elementary School. That was the school where our neighbor, Mrs. Shropshire, taught, so she would drive me to nursery school every morning since my mother had to teach at the high school. I still associate the aroma of Ivory soap with washing hands at nursery school.

When I was four years old, my mother and I took a trip with my aunt and uncle to Chicago. My brother Ernest hadn't been born yet, so I was still an only child. My father was working, so he could not come along with us, and my uncle drove us the whole way there in his blue Buick. We made a special stop to visit President Abraham Lincoln's home in Springfield, Illinois.

Even at that age I knew Lincoln was a very important president and that my family was making a point to drive through Springfield. I had just recently learned how to print my name, and my mother and aunt encouraged me to sign the guestbook at the historic site. Mother allowed me to write my own name and because I had just learned to write, the letters of my full name "TREOPIA CLARA GREEN" spread across two whole pages of the guest book. I was very proud of myself!

***

In 1941 my mother and aunt were part of a group of Dunbar High School teachers who sued the Little Rock School Board for equal pay for Black teachers. They were being paid significantly less than their White counterparts in the school system, and the school board refused to pay them what they were due. Mrs. Sue Cowan Williams, the head of the Dunbar English Department, was chosen to represent the teachers in a class action lawsuit. The teachers collected enough money to pay Mrs. Williams' salary because they knew she would be fired. She was represented by NAACP attorney and future Supreme Court Justice, Thurgood Marshall.

On one of his visits to Little Rock, during the course of the suit, my mother and father were asked to host Thurgood Marshall because there were no hotel accommodations available for Black people at that time. I was just a little girl, but I knew when Mother said Attorney Marshall would be arriving, he was somebody important.

I heard Mother and Daddy say Attorney Marshall was going to fly into Little Rock. Very few people traveled by airplane then, so when I heard that I got excited, feeling certain his plane would land right in our backyard. We had a row of windows across the back of our house, and I stood on a stepstool looking out the window, waiting for his plane to land. I waited there a long time, and then the doorbell rang, and Mother announced, "Attorney Marshall is here." He walked through the front door, no airplane in sight! Many years later, his son and I both served in the Clinton administration, and I had the chance to tell him the story of how his father had "disappointed me"!

I vividly remember overhearing Mother and Auntie talking about the lawsuit, although I didn't understand what they were saying. Eventually, the suit was successful, and more importantly it was one of a series of lawsuits during that era that helped lay the groundwork for the landmark case *Brown v. Board of Education* won by Thurgood Marshall.

***

I went to kindergarten at St. Bartholomew Catholic School. I think it was probably the only kindergarten available to Black children, since public school kindergartens were not standard yet. It was a great experience. At Christmas we participated in Christmas Eve mass at the church. I can remember the lighted candles as we walked down the aisle. It was a beautiful service.

Our teacher had us put on lots of plays, and one of the plays we did was "Snow White." I had the lead role, and the prince was to kiss me on the cheek to wake me up. It was the most exciting thing!

When I was five, my brother Ernest was born, and Mother stopped teaching home economics at Dunbar High School. She stayed out for a couple of years until a friend of hers, who was principal at Stephens, asked her to become a first-grade teacher. And that's what she did for the rest of her teaching career. It was a different school, a different level but she really enjoyed it.

I used to help Mother create bulletin boards and prepare her classroom for the coming year. There are still people in Little Rock who remember her as their first-grade teacher and speak of her fondly. Seeing how much people respected my mother is what inspired me at a young age to become a teacher.

I remember once when I was very young and out shopping with my mother, a young White sales lady looked at my mother and said, "Are you a teacher?" And Mother said, "Yes, why?" The sales lady said, "Well, you look like a teacher, and you act like a teacher, and you talk like a teacher, and I just thought you might be a teacher." That really impressed me as a child. I thought, "Wow, if this is how people respect and recognize teachers, then that's something pretty neat to be."

I remember another instance around that same time, when I was with my mother shopping in a department store. She was buying fabric because she was always making something or sewing a new outfit. The sales lady, a young White woman, said, "What do you *girls* want?" My mother simply turned to me and said, "Treopia, she must be talking to you because you are the only girl here."

Referring to Black women and men as "girls" and "boys" was a common practice at that time, meant to convey their lower status in society. My mother always responded to people in a way that demanded respect, but she did it in a non-confrontational manner. For instance, she had a charge at one of the stores, but she always signed her receipts "Mrs. Green." She never used her first name because she knew if she did, the salesclerk would call her only by her first name instead of the more polite and respectful title "Mrs." My brother always said the salesclerks probably thought her first name was "Mrs."! She was very aware of the ways the Jim Crow system tried to demean people of color, and she found subtle ways to defy the system.

Once when we were grocery shopping in Safeway, a little White boy called Ernest, who was a toddler, the "N" word. My mother simply said, just loud enough for his mother to hear, "It is unfortunate that his vocabulary is so limited, that he uses language like that." Another lesson in diplomacy!

***

My mother would often take me to the theater when I was a child. I saw Duke Ellington, Nat King Cole, and the Sadler's Wells Ballet Company from London, plus many children's theater productions. We would have to sit in the balcony and were not allowed on the main floor, but my mother never said anything about the restriction. I just knew that in the balcony was where we had to sit. It was against the law to sit on the first floor, but we still saw and heard everything that everyone else did.

One time, when I was out shopping with my mother, we went into a department store that had a white porcelain drinking fountain and a black porcelain drinking fountain, side by side. I, of course, wanted a drink and asked my mother which fountain I should use. She replied, "You may choose whichever one you like."

Opportunities for travel, arts, and culture were the kinds of experiences my family wanted us to have growing up. It's hard for me to even begin to enumerate the many experiences they made sure we had, but they did it in such a way that did not enhance the negativity of that period. Yet, even as protective as the adults in my family were, they could not completely shut out the effects of a segregated society.

When I was in kindergarten, I remember my mother took me to the beauty salon to have my hair done for my school play. I had found a picture in a coloring book of a little White girl with straight hair in a pageboy style. I brought that picture with me to show the beautician how I would like my hair to look. But, of course, when the beautician was finished, I had my usual curly ringlets. Well, I looked in the mirror and I cried. I was so disappointed. My hair looked nothing like the girl with the pageboy cut in my picture. There were no pictures of African Americans in coloring books, magazines, or newspapers at that time. I didn't see images of people who looked like me in print.

Another time around that same age, I remember after seeing a picture of a White girl in one of my books, I looked in the mirror and thought to myself, "Maybe I would be pretty, if my nose and lips were keener." Fortunately, it was a fleeting thought, and I never told anyone. My parents did not emphasize physical beauty and were so supportive and encouraging that those damaging messages about my self-image never really took hold. But I wonder about all the Black children who did not have such strong role models? How did it make them feel to not be represented at all, to never see a positive image of themselves in society? My mother and father, somehow without saying it overtly to me and my brothers, made us feel that we were as good as anyone—not better than but as good as.

***

I will never forget when President Truman came to town. The postmistress, Mrs. Robinson, hosted a dinner for him, and my father served the dinner. Daddy told mother to bring me to the garden so that we could see President Truman. Sure enough, the President's car stopped at the drive, and he walked through the garden. Mother and I were sitting on the garden bench, and he stopped and chatted with us. I remember he had on a white Panama hat and white suit because it was summertime.

Although he had believed in segregation as a young man, President Truman's views changed over time, and in 1948 he desegregated the military and federal workforce. Truman was deeply troubled by violent attacks that Black World War II veterans were facing in America when they returned from their service to the country. He was particularly disturbed by the lynchings that happened in 1946 in Georgia when two Black veterans and their wives were pulled from their car and killed by a White mob. President Truman created a committee to investigate the violence and intimidation that Black citizens were enduring.

***

Enforcing poll taxes and literacy tests were ways in the Jim Crow era that Black voters were discouraged from exercising their right to vote. Voting was always something that my mother and father did and that helped us to know how important voting was. I can remember overhearing conversations my parents had talking about "paying the poll tax" in order to vote. Mother would ask Daddy, "Ernest, did you remember to pay your poll tax? Don't forget to pay the poll tax." It was something they had to be aware of and be sure to get done because they were determined to vote.

My aunt had a friend who taught college in Mississippi, and she was a committed voter. In Mississippi the criteria for Black people to vote, was to recite the Preamble of the Constitution. My aunt's friend, who was a professor, went into her polling place wearing a head rag and shuffling and mumbling. When the poll workers told her she would have to recite the preamble, they assumed she would not be able to do it because of how she appeared to them. She wanted to make a point and so she stood up tall, threw her head back, and recited the preamble beautifully from start to finish. After that, the pollsters told all the "Negroes" present that they could vote!

***

Church was a very important part of our lives growing up in Little Rock. Because of Jim Crow laws social activity was strictly confined to our homes, so the church served a very important role in our community. It was like an extension of the family. My Sunday School teachers gave us the same kind of support as our family, community, and school. Speaking opportunities and performances in front of groups all took place in the church. In fact, my public speaking began at church in Sunday School, having to recite Easter poems or Christmas poems.

When I was about eight years old our church hosted the meeting of the African Methodist Episcopal (AME) Bishops Council. Bishops from all over the country, all over the world came to it, and I was asked to give a welcome address. My mother and aunt did not make anything of how important this was, but I practiced my speech until I got it right. I remember being on stage in front of all the bishops to recite it. My mother had made me a very pretty white dress, and at the end of my welcome one of the older bishops gave me a red rose, which I pressed and kept for many years.

Whenever we did recitals and things like that my parents never carried on about it. I can't remember anything they said, but feeling they approved of us and were satisfied was important to us.

On Sunday mornings, Mother made us a lovely breakfast, and we ate together. Then we went to Sunday School and church. My brothers and I used to laugh and say that unless you were dead, you got up and went to church on Sunday! My father attended the largest Baptist church in Little Rock, Mount Zion, and my mother attended the largest AME church, Bethel AME. I was a member of Bethel AME. Two of the Little Rock Nine were also members of Bethel AME Church. Because they were younger, I knew them as children growing up. They and my brother Ernest attended Sunday School and church together.

Our church, Bethel AME, was located on 9th and Broadway, at one end of the block where Black businesses were relegated to in that area of Little Rock. There were two drug stores nearby, so we would walk up and get an ice cream cone after Sunday School before the church service began.

I remember hearing of one horrific incident that happened on the block right across the street from my church. There was a lynching in 1927, years before I was born, and pews were stolen from the church and used to burn the body of the man who was lynched. My grandfather might have known of this event firsthand because he was a member of Bethel AME during that time. My grandfather also became a trustee of the Bethel AME Church, and my Aunt Treopia was the first female trustee.

I would go with Daddy to Mount Zion Baptist occasionally because many of my schoolmates belonged to that church. In the summer we would go there for Vacation Bible School. Then when the Bethel AME Vacation Bible School would take place a week later, we would go to that one. I realized as an adult that it was not only my parents wanting to provide us with a variety of experiences, but also because they were both working, they needed to figure out childcare to make sure we were cared for and doing something productive while they were at work.

I consider myself ecumenical because of my experiences with different denominations growing up. I went to a Catholic kindergarten and a Seventh Day Adventist school for part of first grade. I attended both the Baptist and AME churches of my parents. When I moved to Baltimore, I lived with an elementary school principal and his wife, who had grown up in Little Rock and was a friend of my mother. They went to an Episcopal church, where he was choir director, so I went to church with them. My mother said when I went away to college, "It doesn't matter what kind of church you're affiliated with, just affiliate with some church." Several years after moving to Baltimore to teach, I became a member of Union Baptist Church, where I am still active.

***

My mother was extremely well respected by everyone who knew her. It was important to gain the level of self-respect to where you could use that respect to set things straight when you needed to. My mother had a way of doing this without being confrontational, like how she responded to the white saleslady, who said, "What do you *girls* want?"

The only time I ever say my mother halfway frustrated was one day when we were shopping in Woolworth's, and I wanted to go to the lunch counter. I said to her, "Oh, I'm hungry, can't we stop at the lunch counter to eat?" And I remember Mother, kind of under her breath saying to herself, "Everybody else, I don't care how scrappy they look or how ignorant they are, can go to the lunch counter." But she didn't say it to me, I just kind of overheard her muttering it to herself. What she said to me was, "We will go home and have lunch."

That was the only time I ever witnessed my mother reacting negatively to the situations she had to go through because of Jim Crow laws. It was the only time I ever heard her even respond in a way that I knew that it was upsetting to her. That experience shows the everyday cruelty of the Jim Crow system—how frustrating and demeaning it was for people of color.

I will never forget that experience, the two of us by the lunch counter in Woolworth's Five and Dime. A Woolworth's lunch counter was ultimately where the first sit-ins took place in North Carolina twenty years later, a key moment in the civil rights movement. One of the people involved in the sit-ins told my brother that they were inspired by what he did when he and the Nine integrated Central High School in Little Rock. We never talked about segregation and Jim Crow growing up, but I knew that my mother was happy when civil rights laws began to evolve.

***

My elementary school, Gibbs, was next door to Dunbar which housed the junior high and high school. It was inspiring to know that someday, you would go to the "big school." I went to summer school and ended up being ahead two grade levels, so I was always among the youngest in my class.

Mother would always make gorgeous clothes for me, and I remember I would come home from school and say to her, "Mother, I'm going to be in a program for the assembly, the day after tomorrow," and she would always make me a new outfit. She must have been tired from teaching, but she would take the time to make something pretty for me to wear. Our neighbor across the street, Mrs. Jackson, didn't have children, and she was the one I would always go to show my new outfit. She would always make a fuss and talk about how pretty it was.

We did not have a gym or physical education facilities at my school, and the local public swimming pools were closed to Black people. My mother would take us regularly to the zoo at Fair Park, and the public pool was in the same area so we would walk by the pool to go to the zoo and see White people coming in and having a good time, but we knew that we couldn't go in. That's why I didn't swim as a child, because there was no place to learn. Finally, Gilliam Park opened when I was a junior or senior in high school. My younger brother Scott learned to swim there and always loved it. But those were the kinds of experiences I missed.

I went to Girl Scouts Camp every summer at Camp Clearfork in Hot Springs, Arkansas. It was a beautiful, wooded area and there was a lake you could swim in, but I would only get my feet wet. I wasn't about to jump into the lake!

***

When I was seven years old and my brother Ernest was two, my youngest brother Scott was born on December 23, 1943. I always said that made me an undeniable believer in Santa Claus because on Christmas Eve my older cousin Mildred, whom I adored, spent the night with me and Ernest. My mother was still in the hospital having just given birth and my father always served this family on Christmas Eve, every year, so he was working. And yet the next morning, Christmas Day, when we awoke, everything I had wanted was under the Christmas tree. I knew that there was a Santa Claus. Nobody could tell me my parents did that because my parents weren't there! The cookies we had left by the tree for Santa Claus had been eaten, so Santa came and brought all our things.

We went to visit Mother and our new baby brother Scott in the hospital on Christmas Day. I remember the weather was icy and cold, but we were excited about the new addition to the family. I don't remember suffering any kind of negative feelings when another sibling was born—the love was just spread around and expanded.

At the age of three, Scott contracted polio. I still remember vividly the day we noticed a kind of limp when he was walking. Mother made an appointment with the pediatrician, and she took Scott to the doctor. I was standing at the back window waiting for her to come home, and I saw Mother coming from the bus stop without Scott and she was crying, something I had never seen before in my life. When she came inside, she told my father that when the doctor examined Scott, he determined he had polio and immediately put Scott in the hospital.

That was earthshaking for our family. This was before the polio vaccine was available. We knew of President Roosevelt who had polio and was in a wheelchair. A common treatment for the disease was an early respirator machine called an "iron lung." Fortunately, my brother Scott did not need this treatment and didn't suffer paralysis, but he had to stay in the hospital by himself for about a week when he was only three years old. Since Jim Crow segregation laws were rampant at that time, I have always wondered how he was treated by the White hospital staff. Of course, my family was there whenever they were allowed to visit, but they were not able to be there with him all the time.

***

When I was about seven or eight years old, after church one Sunday, we went to General MacArthur Park to hear a concert being held under the gazebo. When we arrived and had just stepped onto the curb of the sidewalk leading to the gazebo, a policeman met us and said, "We don't allow coloreds to listen to this music." I remember my mother and father turned to us and my mother said, "We will find something else nice to do this afternoon." And we turned around and walked away.

My mother and father would never respond in a confrontational way. Not only was it dangerous to do so, but it also just wasn't their way. I don't remember feeling upset about it at the time it happened because my parents knew how to handle things so they would not be hurtful to us. That was just a way of life. I didn't realize how negative it was until I became grown. But when I think now as an adult about the self-control that must have taken, I'm amazed. That response took a lot of poise and dignity.

I had gone to the park many times before that experience. The art museum was in MacArthur Park, and my mother was a great person for making sure that we visited museums, and as a result, I came to love museums. But to demonstrate the impact that had on me as a child, when I was home for the 60th Anniversary of the Little Rock Nine, a few years ago, the hotel I was staying in was just three blocks from General MacArthur Park, and I realized I had not gone back there in over fifty years.

Subconsciously I just never wanted to go back there after that experience. Even when I drove past the park (I had rented a car for that trip), I had a funny feeling in the pit of my stomach. The point is you don't forget these things, even though you eventually get over them. That MacArthur Park experience was my most memorable Jim Crow experience growing up during segregation. In fact, I can still see it. I can visualize it now.

Our family really protected us from having a lot of negative experiences, and of course, we didn't realize it then. Many, many people have had more serious experiences than I have had. I've been fortunate. Those who have had even worse experiences, you wonder how they have survived psychologically. The more I think about my mother and father and aunt and grandfather and others, I have to believe they were pretty strong people. They didn't talk about what we couldn't do. My family always encouraged us and talked about what was expected of us and what we should do—in spite of.

***

Several years ago, I spoke to a group of high school students and shared some experiences related to segregation and growing up during the Jim Crow era. I told them about sitting in the back of the bus, being relegated to the balcony at concerts and plays, and for some movie theaters not being able to go at all. One boy kept asking, "Well, why did you do that?" It was hard for him to understand that this was the law back then. I finally said to him, "I don't expect you to understand, but I expect you to accept what I'm telling you because I'm sharing my lived experience with you."

It's difficult for young people to understand what that period was. But we knew what the rules were, and at that time the Ku Klux Klan was alive and well. When I was a little older and could read the newspaper, I remember reading in the *Arkansas State Press*, the "colored paper," almost every week, about someone being lynched—hung from a tree. I can remember the *State Press* had articles almost every week about a lynching and I can remember seeing the pictures of people who were lynched. The lynchings occurred primarily in the Deep South states of Louisiana, Georgia, Mississippi, and Alabama. I didn't experience that kind of violence myself growing up in Little Rock, but to this day I don't know some of the things my mother and father might have gone through.

The *Arkansas State Press* was the only paper in Arkansas that had news and pictures about Black people. The other papers, the White-run papers, only covered statistical data about Black people such as births and deaths. The *State Press* was one of the few Black newspapers published at that time. Others were: *The Chicago Defender*, *The Pittsburg Courier*, and the Baltimore and Washington DC *Afro-American*. My family subscribed to several Black newspapers, as well as the main daily newspaper in Little Rock.

***

I remember the day President Franklin D. Roosevelt said America was at war. My mother was feeding my baby brother and she was sitting on the side of her bed. We were listening to the radio and a newsflash came on and interrupted our program. It was President Roosevelt saying Pearl Harbor had been bombed. I didn't know much about what that meant, but I remember my mother had a very somber look on her face. I knew it was not good.

During World War II everything was rationed, and stamps were issued for groceries and gas. I remember my mother getting up early to get in line at Gus Blass Department Store to buy silk hose because they were rationed too. Chocolate candy was scarce, but we had a friend who was in the Women's Army Corps (WACS), and she had access to the army post store. Once she sent me a box of Hershey's chocolates. That was a rarity.

My mother was very particular about our not eating too much candy and would only let us have a little bit. One night I slipped one of the Hershey chocolate bars to bed with me, fell asleep on it, and it melted in my hair. The next morning, I was in serious trouble. I don't remember what the outcome was, but I do remember I never did that again! My hair was quite long at the time, and it was a sticky mess.

During World War II a Black army lieutenant, Lt. Faulkner, and his wife were assigned to Camp Robinson in North Little Rock. There was no housing available for Black officers on the base because of segregation, so my mother provided our guest room for them to stay in temporarily while the military located housing. They left an indelible impression on me.

My brother, Ernest, was a baby at that time, and the Faulkners had a baby about the same age. That made it easier for my mother to agree to the arrangement. Mrs. Faulkner was gorgeous. Her husband would bring her candy occasionally and roses, and she would share her candy with me, which I enjoyed.

Lt. Faulkner invited our family to be his guests for Thanksgiving dinner at Camp Robinson, and we were picked up in an army jeep. It was so exciting to ride in the army jeep! We had dinner in the Officer's Dining Hall. I remember we had Oreo cookies for dessert.

I learned many years later that the Faulkners divorced, and Mrs. Faulkner became known as Carrole Drake, actress and model. She then married Billy Eckstine, the famous jazz singer and band leader, and they had children. She was in the movie *Band of Angels* in 1957 with Clark Gable and Sidney Poitier. I will never forget my time spent with her.

My mother often took me to the movies—we only went to musicals. We were at a movie in the Rialto theater, in North Little Rock, when a newsflash came on the screen announcing that the war had ended. The crowd erupted in cheers. I had seen newspaper pictures of the horrors of the Holocaust concentration camps, and we were overjoyed that the war was over. I remember we caught the bus to go home after the movie, and people were in the street celebrating, and cars were honking; it was just a magical moment.

***

My mother and aunt were very active in many different clubs and organizations, including the NAACP and YWCA. They were not allowed to use meeting spaces at hotels for their gatherings and events. In spite of this, there was no lack of social experiences. Social events such as teas, weddings, and organization meetings were all held in homes. This meant that families experienced the utmost in hostessing.

My mother and aunt were members of the first African American sorority chapters in Arkansas, Sigma Gamma Rho, and my mother would host sorority meetings at our house. Several Dunbar High School teachers were also part of this sorority. My brother recalled that it was his job to make sure the baseboards were spotless before they met at our house! I recently found out that my mother and aunt were founding members of the sorority's mother chapter in Arkansas. They never talked about themselves or their achievements, so I never knew the depth of their involvement.

My parents were part of the Appomattox Club in Little Rock. The members were doctors, lawyers, and teachers in the Black community; leaders of the community. There were Appomattox Clubs founded by African Americans for social and civic involvement in cities across the United States, including Washington DC, Chicago, and Oakland, beginning in the 1920s. The clubs were named for the Civil War Battle of Appomattox when Confederate General Robert E. Lee surrendered to Union General Ulysses S. Grant. When the club met at our home, my parents didn't drink alcohol, but Daddy would have stored several bottles of liquor, and he would bring it out for that meeting, for those people who did want a drink. After, it would go back under lock and key until the next time.

I can remember times when mother was talking with another adult, I would ask her, "Mother, what are you talking about?" And her response always was, "We're talking about the dangers that are threatening the Republic." That was her way of shutting me up, but I realize now it's quite possible that's exactly what they were talking about. The phrase is strikingly similar to the title of the abolitionist Frederick Douglass's most famous speech "Sources of Danger to the Republic," where he calls for the need for Black people to have equal voting rights.

***

In 1947 my Aunt Treopia received her master's degree in Education from Atlanta University, the only HBCU to offer graduate degrees. I was eleven, and I traveled by train, by myself, to her graduation. One of the largest employers of Black men, at that time, was the railroad. My family had friends who were Pullman Car porters, or waiters in the dining car. They would tell my mother, "Don't worry about Treopia. We'll take good care of her." At dinnertime, they would come for me and take me to the dining car and usually I was the only person of color in the dining car.

I remember this particular trip because we went through Birmingham, Alabama, late at night, and I was scared to death because it was the period when Black people were being dragged from vehicles and train cars and lynched. I was so scared with the train going through Birmingham that night, I couldn't sleep. I remember sitting in my train seat, holding my little purse close. I don't think I slept at all that night.

When I arrived in Atlanta safely, my aunt met me at the station. I had a guidebook about Georgia, and Stone Mountain was on a list of sites to see around Atlanta. I didn't know much about it but was curious, so I mentioned it to my aunt. I remember her response was something like, "That's not a place we want to visit." She didn't have to elaborate—I knew what that meant. What I didn't know at the time was that Stone Mountain was the symbolic birthplace of the modern Ku Klux Klan movement in 1915 and the site of a giant rock carving to commemorate Confederate leaders.

We attended the graduation ceremony, and on the train ride home, several of my aunt's fellow teachers also were returning to Little Rock. When we lined up at the station to board the train there were at least twenty Black people waiting to get on the train. I knew the section for Black people had only eight seats. I did not want my aunt and her friends to have to stand on the train, so as soon as the conductor arrived, I remember scooting up to the front of the line, giving him my ticket, and then running down the walkway, jumping on the train, and sitting in four seats. I sat in the middle of two and put my feet on the other two facing seats to save them for my aunt and her friends.

On the train, there was a burgundy velvet curtain that separated the "Black seats" from the rest of the car. You knew that if you didn't get those seats, you probably would not be allowed to sit in the other part, even if there were seats available. Those were the kinds of situations we had to deal with during the Jim Crow era.

***

As a child I liked to draw and sketch, and I was interested in pursuing a career in the arts, whether it was ballet, or later a fashion designer. But it seemed impossible to me because art and drawing classes were not available. I would have loved to be able to take art courses, but there wasn't enough funding in the budget at our schools for that. One year my mother signed me up for a correspondence course in art, and I received lessons in the mail, but that way of learning didn't work for me.

We had excellent teachers, but like most schools for Black children in the Jim Crow South, our school was underfunded and did not have the same resources that the White schools had. In fact, many Black high schools did not have the funding for science labs, gyms, or arts and foreign language classes. We were fortunate at Dunbar to have a strong theater department and some foreign language classes. We were also fortunate to have community members who could offer music and dance opportunities.

There were three Black piano teachers in town, and each would have a recital every spring. I took piano lessons for twelve years from Mrs. Campbell. My parents never allowed me to play anything but classical music. That is why, even now, my radios at home and in my car are only tuned to the classical station. That's all I like to listen to.

Art Porter, who was a couple of grades ahead of me at Dunbar, took music lessons from Mrs. Hazel Hynson, another of the piano teachers in our community. Art went on to become a famous jazz musician and band leader, as did his son, Art Porter, Jr.

I took ballet from my grandfather's stepdaughter who was from Chicago. She taught dance in their home on Saturdays, and I loved it. I learned to dance in toe shoes "en pointe." We had recitals every year, and I have a photo of myself in my tutu, which Mother made, wearing my toe shoes. Like many little girls, I dreamed of becoming a ballerina one day. But I dropped that idea because there was nobody who looked like me that did that.

I have loved my career in education, but I can't help but wonder what life might have been like if I'd had more career choices.

Fortunately, however, when I taught kindergarten, I was able to incorporate my love of art, classical music, theater, and dance in the lessons I designed for my students.

***

I never had a job while I was growing up. I remember when I was in junior high or high school, I said something to my mother about working in the summer, getting a summer job, and my mother said, "Your job is to do well in school, that's your work."

My brothers and I knew we were expected to do well all the time, but I never remember my parents saying, "I want you to bring home all A's." We knew we needed to do the very best that we could because they would be disappointed otherwise. The worst thing we could do would be to disappoint our parents. Mother's smile, her encouragement, Daddy's encouragement; that was all we needed.

My parents knew education was the way to have the kind of life we would want to live. They also wanted us to be of service to our community. I volunteered at day camp and did other things like that. One of my mother's philosophies was: you're only as good as you are to other people. Helping other people and being of service to others is what makes you a better person.

My family was able to rear us to always do our best and not to be resentful. I remember once when I was in junior high school, I achieved something in school that I thought was outstanding, and I told my mother about it. She listened and she said, "That's very good, but remember you can always do better." She never bragged about what we did, but we always knew we were expected to do everything as well as we possibly could. Her approval was implicit, it was understood and always so strong. I knew how she felt from her reaction, and the care and attention she gave me.

My ballerina days. Mother made my tutu.

Dancing—a career goal never realized!

Pauline, Rose, Ann, Me + Sidney

My friends and I serving as hostesses at a Sunday afternoon tea. I was in high school.

In my Easter bonnet trimmed by Mother.

FOUR

HIGH SCHOOL YEARS

I was young for my class, and in terms of dating and those things teenagers look forward to, regrettably I was hampered by the position of my aunt at the high school. Aunt Treopia was a fixture at Dunbar. She was the high school counselor and had been the Dean of Girls before that. She had also taught history and a course called "Planning for Your Future." She was very well-respected and very strict. Everybody was scared of her, which meant some were also scared of me!

"Auntie" was what I called her at home and "Mrs. Gravelly" at school. Whenever she would order new standardized tests, she would have me take them. I was her guinea pig, which was actually a good exercise for me because I got used to taking standardized tests and never minded doing it.

I remember my aunt talking about the teachings of Mahatma Gandhi from India. She was very fond of his efforts and an admirer of his philosophy of non-violent resistance, as was Dr. Martin Luther King, Jr.

Auntie and Uncle had a daughter who died two years before I was born. Later they adopted a daughter, Mildred, who I grew up with as a cousin. Several students who were from rural areas and whose families wanted them to get a high school education at Dunbar also lived with my aunt and uncle. These students would help keep the house in exchange for room and board.

I adored my cousin Mildred. She was very nice to me and took me under her wing. Mildred used to draw and sketch a lot, and I think I picked that up from her. Mildred attended Wiley College, an HBCU in Marshall, Texas, to become a teacher. When she would come home my mother would make gorgeous clothes for her to bring back to college. She was married at my aunt's house when I was still in high school. My mother made me a dress of blue silk crepe and let me wear silk hose (for the first time). I was Mildred's only attendant. I remember crying at her wedding—to this day I don't know why I was crying! Her husband lived in Little Rock, and they settled there. She followed in my aunt and mother's footsteps teaching for many years at several elementary schools.

***

When I was younger, I would always have a pretty plaid dress to wear on the first day of school. I can remember some of the dresses in detail. One year J.C. Penney had a sale, and Mother bought two dresses, but that was rare. Other than that, the only times we went to the clothing departments were when I was graduating from high school and preparing for the senior prom.

I remember on several occasions Mother used to say that "labels don't mean anything; it's how a garment looks that's important." We grew up understanding that labels were irrelevant, and that cost did not determine the quality of clothing.

M. M. Cohn was the "high end" department store in Little Rock that carried expensive designer creations. On display was an evening gown designed by Christian Dior, the top French designer of that era. The gown was white tulle with ruffles all over and was just stunning. While Mother examined the construction of the gown, I sketched the gown. And that was the gown she made for my senior prom.

***

Our high school football team used the Central High School stadium on Friday nights, so we would have to walk by Central to get to the stadium, which was in the back of the school. When it was our turn to use the stadium, the White students were gone, so there was never any interaction between students of different races. You couldn't help but notice this enormous, gorgeous school that was Central. But at that time, I know, for me, there was never a desire or even a thought of ever going there. That didn't even cross my mind because you knew there were White schools, and there were Black schools. End of story.

Dunbar High School did not have as many resources as a school like Central. The Little Rock school system finally allocated funds to build a gym during my senior year and that was the first time we had physical education. We had second-hand books that came to us from Central. Many of them had writing in them. But that didn't make a difference, we were given the tools and were expected to excel. The teaching at Dunbar was at such a high caliber. The focus was on excellence, and the support all students received was consistent.

I think some of our Dunbar teachers could have been CEOs of Fortune 500 companies had they been born in a later era. At that time teaching was one of the highest aspirations college-educated Black men and women could have, so the quality of people we had for teachers was outstanding. Many of the teachers had advanced degrees. Our chemistry teacher had a PhD in chemistry. His son went on to become head of the Chemistry Department at the U.S. Naval Academy in Annapolis, Maryland.

Miss Copeland was the drama teacher at Dunbar. The plays she directed were wonderful. I remember my cousin Mildred was "Carmen" for one of her productions, and my mother making her costume with a black lace mantilla.

We had a "Negro History Week," and although we did not learn about events like the massacre in Tulsa, our history teacher made sure that we learned about prominent Black people like George Washington Carver and Frederick Douglass. It was the kind of school community that nurtured us and supported us in everything we did. We could not have had a more excellent school experience even though the physical resources were limited.

***

Many Dunbar teachers went away for six weeks in the summer to universities in the North, such as the University of Iowa or Minnesota, to earn graduate credits for their teaching certificates. Because they were not allowed to take classes at southern universities, the school districts incurred the additional expense to send them North instead. There was so much money, time, and effort put into keeping people separate during the Jim Crow era.

Because my mother had children to care for, she could not afford to go away for six weeks. Eventually the University of Arkansas began offering graduate classes in trailers in Little Rock for Black teachers, on the weekend. Mother completed the work for her master's degree in 1951.

I was standing with her at the door when the postman came with a box from the University of Arkansas. When Mother opened the box, there was a tassel and hood, her diploma, and a letter that congratulated her for completing her work but telling her that it was not the time for her to come to campus to participate in the commencement.

My mother read the letter and then she handed it to me to read. When I gave it back to her, she crumpled it and threw it in the trash and walked away. I knew how hurt she was, but of course, she never said anything. That happened in '51, and I can still see the hurt in her eyes from that day.

***

I don't remember any conversation with my parents that dwelled on what we could not do. The important thing from their perspective was to take what you had and do the best with it. That attitude has really supported me through adulthood.

I think they knew how to raise us this way, knew that children needed to feel that sense of security, to become confident adults, because they were more mature and older when they had children. They knew what the score was and knew what their ambitions were for us.

We emerged as adults with an awareness of our capability, confident in our self-worth. The knowledge that we were as good as, did not support a feeling of superiority in us—it protected us from wrongly believing ourselves to be inferior. It made us believe in ourselves—in spite of.

My high school, Dunbar, was built around the same time as Central. The school board spent $400,000 to build Dunbar but ran out of funding to complete the project because of the $1.5 million spent constructing Central. Families had to find private funding to finish building Dunbar.

"Big Treopia" (Mrs. Gravelly) working with a student and "Little Treopia" helping at the filing cabinet. My mother made the suit: navy and white checked wool with a navy braid-trimmed collar.

My senior yearbook photo. I had a wonderful high school experience at Dunbar and graduated in 1952. I was fifteen when I graduated.

FIVE

COLLEGE YEARS

I turned sixteen the summer after I graduated from high school in 1952 and started my first year of college at Hampton Institute in Virginia that fall.

Before I left for college, my aunt gave me a trip to Chicago for my sixteenth birthday present. Chicago was in the North which meant I could eat in restaurants, which I could not do in Little Rock. We stayed with a girlhood friend of my aunt and mother's from Little Rock and her husband, a dentist. We saw *Porgy and Bess* at the Chicago Opera House, and it was a magnificent production with Cab Calloway, William Warfield, and Leontyne Price. One day, after the opera, we went to a Walgreen's Drugstore on Indiana Avenue on the South Side and saw Cab Calloway there. I got his autograph, and he was very gracious. I was, of course, in awe!

On that trip we also visited the offices of Johnson Publishing Company and that was a revelation to me. Mr. Johnson, a native Arkansan, published *Ebony* magazine, which was the first and foremost publication about Black people. The editor-in-chief was from Arkansas and his editor was one of my aunt's former students at Dunbar. My family subscribed to the magazine, so I read it every month.

We visited the offices and were given the "cook's tour." I had a chance to meet people, whom I had read about. There was a column dedicated to cooking and recipes, and I remember meeting Freda DeKnight, author of the column. That was so exciting! *Ebony* was really the only existing Black magazine at that time. That was also the first time I saw Black models.

Growing up, until my teenage years, the only standard of beauty was White beauty. The very few Black models and actresses in the media were light skinned with keener lips and noses, like my favorite actresses of the day Lena Horne or Dorothy Dandridge. Fashion magazines that featured Black models would even try to make their skin look lighter when they processed the photos. Our homecoming queens in college and high school tended to fit that mold. Recently, my childhood neighbor told me her older brother (my classmate) always thought I was pretty—I never knew that! I remember once having the fleeting thought as I looked in the mirror, "If only my nose were keener, I would be pretty." I didn't express that to my mother because she would have scolded me. My family never emphasized physical features as a standard of beauty; instead it was the way you acted and your attitudes. That was the measuring stick for beauty.

It wasn't until *Ebony* magazine, and later *Jet* magazine, began to be published that a wide variety of pictures of Black people—models, actors, musicians, and community leaders—were featured. *Ebony* did several stories about my brother Ernest. Before those publications, we never saw those images because the mainstream media did not portray them.

Little Rock's main newspapers, the *Gazette* and the *Democrat*, included birth and death statistics, but did not print news of substance about things happening in Black communities. This is why Black-owned newspapers like the *Arkansas State Press* were so important. Black parents really had to work hard to make sure that children felt worthwhile and that they could and should accomplish a lot, because that was definitely not supported in the world as a whole.

It's difficult for one to imagine this era conceptually if they haven't personally experienced it. We knew what the rules were. We were fortunate that our family consisted of people who didn't talk about what you couldn't do but provided opportunities that allowed us to excel. This practically freed us from bearing the burden of the system that tried to constrain our dreams and ambitions. We were able to grow up secure in ourselves.

***

The college I attended, Hampton Institute, was and still is one of the most recognized historically Black colleges in America. It was founded in 1868, soon after the Civil War ended slavery, by a White Union Army general, Samuel Chapman Armstrong. There were quite a few people, particularly Quakers, who were interested in supporting education for newly freed slaves. Until the Emancipation Proclamation was created, it was against the law for slaves to learn to read and write. On campus, there is a tree called "Emancipation Oak," and it is a tree that is still standing, under which the Emancipation Proclamation was read to the slaves to let them know they were free.

Originally called Hampton Institute, it has since become Hampton University. Like many historically Black colleges and universities (HBCUs), Hampton was initially created to train teachers to teach ex-slaves. It also had a manual component where young men could learn trades and a farming component when it was founded. Booker T. Washington is one of the most famous Hampton alums.

Dr. Martin Luther King Jr.'s mother, Alberta Williams King, graduated from Hampton in 1924. This is the same year that my mother graduated from Wilberforce College in Ohio.

When my mother was in college, she spent a summer at Hampton Institute. She would reminisce about it when I was a child, and I would listen to her describe the campus, on the water, near the Chesapeake Bay. I had this fascination for water and the seashore—things that did not exist in Little Rock. Whenever my mother talked about Hampton, I envisioned this as a possible college destination. At that time, options were limited because White southern universities did not accept Black students. I knew I would go to an HBCU, because they were an important part of my family's experience. When my classmates and I finished high school, those of us who planned to go away to college would choose between HBCUs like Hampton or Tuskegee in Alabama, Spelman and Morehouse in Atlanta, Wilberforce in Ohio, Fisk in Tennessee, or Howard University in Washington DC, to name a few.

When it came time, I applied to Hampton, with my family's encouragement, and was accepted. Because my mother and aunt were such well-known teachers in our community, sometimes people said things that made it seem like I was riding my family's coattails. Little Rock was small enough that it seemed everyone thought they knew something about you, and I think subconsciously one of the reasons I wanted to live away from Little Rock was to demonstrate that I could do things on my own.

There was an upperclassman, from Little Rock, enrolled at Hampton. Her parents belonged to the same church as my father, so I knew her quite well. We traveled together, by train, on the Missouri-Pacific Railroad, to start my freshman year. The train ride was thirty-six hours and lots of fun. Our car was always full of students, primarily from Texas, traveling to White colleges: William and Mary, University of Virginia, and others. This time, we rode together in the same car. Evidently some railroads had begun to desegregate.

When I was at Hampton, most of the other students were from the East Coast, particularly the Carolinas. There were also a few students from Texas. One of the Texas students' rooms was right across from mine when we were freshmen. Her father was a doctor, and she arrived with a gorgeous wardrobe. That's what made it so wonderful—to meet people whose backgrounds and hometowns were completely different from mine. I still stay in touch with one of my classmates who was from South Carolina and now lives in Michigan.

My friend Joyce, whom I had known in Little Rock, entered Hampton about the same time I did, as her parents both assumed positions at Hampton. We were good friends growing up—my mother had even made matching dresses for us when we were young. Her father was head of Dunbar Junior College at one time, but the family moved when he became dean at an HBCU in Oklahoma, Langston University. When I was twelve or thirteen years old, I visited Joyce and her family in Oklahoma. It was a great experience for me. A highlight was my trip with Joyce and her parents, to visit Stilwell, Oklahoma, an important part of the Cherokee Nation.

I tell young people today to take every opportunity to experience other people whose backgrounds are unlike yours, because that's how you learn to appreciate other people. You realize that there are different ways of doing things, and those differences do not define whether something is "good" or "not good."

I didn't feel homesick when I went away to college because I was accustomed to traveling. I smile when I hear about students going to college now, and parents driving them to school and going to visit them. When I went away to college that was not going to happen, but I was so excited about college that homesickness never occurred for me. Also, I was in a dorm with other freshmen who were away from home, so we were company for each other. It was a good atmosphere at Hampton.

While at Hampton, I looked forward to spending the Thanksgiving holiday with my cousins, Zelma and Clara, my father's sister Clara's daughters, in Washington, DC. Going home for that holiday was out of the question, Little Rock was too far. We always had a lively discussion at dinner, with their "play brother," Don Young, a lawyer, who was an alum of Lincoln University in Pennsylvania. Zelma graduated from Howard University, so our talk was always about which was the best HBCU—Hampton, Howard, or Lincoln. Sometimes I won!

The "dorm mother" my freshman year was always interested in the many boxes I received from home. I would tell her about mother's talent for sewing and design and would sometimes share the peanut brittle candy that Mother occasionally sent. I would also talk about my wonderful experiences growing up in Little Rock. To my surprise, several years after I graduated, I learned that she and her family had moved to Little Rock, where she began teaching. I like to think that maybe I had something to do with her decision to relocate.

In that era, before cell phones and contemporary technology, Mother would send me a special delivery letter that I would receive on Sunday, and most Sundays I would call home. That's how we kept in touch and how I would share all the things I was doing in college. I still have a scrapbook that I started my freshman year, with items that are reminiscent of my college experience.

People have asked me if I had a nickname growing up, and the answer is, "Absolutely not!" I was named for my aunt, for whom everyone had the deepest respect, and would never, ever desecrate her name. It wasn't until college that I acquired a nickname. Several of my classmates called me "Tre," but nobody growing up in Little Rock would dare call me that!

***

When I was still a high school senior, I entered a national essay contest sponsored by the National Urban League, and I won. However, I didn't receive that award until I had already started my freshman year at Hampton. I was in swimming class (in order to graduate you had to pass swimming), when I got the call from the college president's office.

The swimming instructor alerted me and said, "President Moron called and said that the president of the National Urban League in New York is coming down to present you with a scholarship prize for the essay contest. They are going to have a special assembly." I was dripping wet, and the assembly was going to be held that afternoon!

I rushed to my dorm room to get ready and tried to dress appropriately. In my college yearbook there is a picture of me receiving the award. I wore a nice skirt and top that my mother had made. It was truly exciting, and a special experience for me—and I have a picture in my yearbook to prove it.

***

Every August, when I was in college, my mother and I would shop for fabrics and then spend most of the month making my wardrobe for the year. We had a screened-in side porch and since this was before the days of central air, Mother would move the sewing machine out there and we would sit on the porch, on the cool side of the house. I would help with the sewing by cutting, pinning, basting, and doing other things to help. I think the more complicated the pattern, the more she enjoyed using it. The challenge was fun for her. Mother would use a Vogue pattern, but would always do something to individualize it, to make it special and unique.

It was a tradition I had with my mother to do this every summer. People knew that she would be sewing that month and neighbors would walk down the sidewalk, which was right outside the screened porch and would stop to chat. That was something she and I enjoyed doing together every year. She would also send me boxes of new clothes she made for me throughout the year while I was away at college. I found out later who the model was for my dresses while she fitted them—my younger brother, Scott who was about my height, at nine years old! He told me, many years later, that he did not enjoy that experience!

When I would come home to Little Rock in the summer from college, I modeled in fashion shows, held in churches, sponsored by one of my mother's organizations. Years later, after desegregation, we were able to conduct the fashion shows in the Lafayette Hotel, considered one of the nicest in Little Rock. When I finally saw inside the hotel, it was a bit shabby and did not fulfill my expectations. I remember thinking, "Is this what they've been keeping us out of?"

***

I once had aspirations of becoming a dress designer. There were no Black designers that I knew of, but I daydreamed about taking Paris by storm. In fact, Hampton did have a major in dress design, but it was eliminated two years before I was ready to go to college. After giving that career some thought, I decided it best to consider other options. "You can't be what you don't see"!

That was the same way I felt when I took dancing lessons. I had a fleeting thought, "What if I could be a ballerina?" But, again, at that time the models to look up to just didn't exist. It's so important to see other people like you in positions that you could aspire to. Because of the way things were, I assumed there were certain things I would not be able to do.

My mother and father never discouraged me from wanting to become a dress designer, but somehow, I realized that if I wanted to maintain any ability to eat and have a place to live, I'd better rethink my ambitions. Becoming a teacher was it!

Of course, teaching was the profession within my family, and I never regretted my decision to become a teacher. Now, the options are much greater, and I can't help but imagine sometimes, what if more opportunities had been available when I was dreaming of a career back then?

But I'm glad that my life has provided the opportunity to experience all these things—even life during the Jim Crow era when options for Black people were so limited. It may sound strange to say this, but I feel privileged in a certain way to have been born at a time when things were totally different. My life has spanned so many changes and different periods through history, and I have been blessed with many extraordinary experiences.

***

During my sophomore year at Hampton, I took the train home for Christmas vacation, and when I got off the train at the station in Little Rock, I didn't see Daddy. Mother and Daddy were always there to meet me, but it was just my mother and our family friend, the nurse who lived up the street from us, standing there on the platform.

"Where's Daddy?" I asked, and my mother said very quietly, "Your daddy passed away yesterday."

When I heard her words, I dropped my hard Samsonite suitcase, and it fell to the floor of the station platform. I can still hear the sound it made as it hit the concrete platform.

They couldn't get in touch with me because I was already on the train on my way home when he passed suddenly on December 17, 1953. Daddy evidently hadn't been feeling well, so he went to the Veterans Hospital, and he never came home. We never learned the exact cause of death. He was the type who wouldn't have complained if he was ill.

He died when he was sixty-five years old, having worked twelve to sixteen-hour days, sometimes seven days a week, for forty years. He never complained, but he worked all day at the post office doing janitorial work and then worked almost every evening serving parties. I have always thought he worked himself to death.

My father's funeral was held just a few days before Christmas, and my mother made sure that we experienced Christmas as we would have had Daddy been there. The more I think about it now, I don't know how she did it. We had a Christmas tree, gifts from "Santa", and Christmas dinner. Mother made sure that my brothers, who were younger than I, would experience our traditional Christmas. To me, that was the epitome of strength.

I don't remember much about the funeral, but during that time the body would lie in state at the home. My mother never broke down in front of us. Her ability to keep going, to keep living in the midst of our tragedy, showed us at our young ages—I was seventeen, Ernest was twelve, and Scott was ten—that life could go on even with the loss our father. I remember sometime after Daddy passed, I asked Mother if she was going to get married again, and she said she had a wonderful marriage for nearly thirty years and that she wouldn't marry again.

***

During college, my parents paid for all my tuition, all the expenses, and I never had to work while I was in school. When my mother passed thirty-two years later, my brothers and I were at the lawyer's office to settle her affairs, and for the first time we viewed our parent's financial details. We saw what her salary was as a teacher, and it was very modest. My father's salary at the post office had been minimal as well, which was why he worked his second job serving dinner parties. We don't know how they managed, but Mother was a manager par excellence, very skillful at stretching the money we had. We never did without.

Because my parents were so proficient at managing their money and resources, the sudden loss of my father, and the income he provided, was not the devastating turning point in our family's story that it might have been. I was able to return to college and complete my education. My mother and brothers were able to stay in our family home in Little Rock. In material ways we didn't miss a beat, but we felt my father's absence deeply. Our family life would never be quite the same again.

***

After my father passed, I stayed in Little Rock for half the next semester, so I needed to take summer school to catch up to be able to graduate my senior year with my class. That summer I stayed with the college chaplain and his wife, Reverend and Mrs. Bodine, who were White. (Hampton had a wonderful, diversified faculty.) I was co-chair of the Student Christian Association, and Reverend Bodine was the faculty sponsor. Mrs. Bodine taught psychology and physiology.

The Bodines lived in faculty housing, near the water. The house was located near a footbridge that led to town and we used to walk into town. The town of Hampton was very small at that time, and we could walk everywhere. It was so much fun. That summer was very enjoyable. I was seventeen turning eighteen that year, and the Bodines gave me a surprise birthday party.

One of my summer school classes was psychology, and the Bodines had a dog and had just gotten a new dog. I used the older dog as the psychological study for one of my papers. That dog exhibited all the signs of maladjustment and trauma with the addition of the new pet!

I remember something else fondly from that summer. This was 1955, not long after the Brown v. Board of Education ruling, so integration was a subject that had come up nationally. When Mrs. Bodine and I would go to a store in Hampton to go shopping—she was a real jokester— she would yell across the store, "Treopia! I think later on we should do such-and-such" and she would say something we planned to do later. Of course, I played along and enjoyed it, calling my answer across the store back to her. She did it in a way to agitate people because they were not used to seeing Black and White people socializing together as friends. So, she made it public like that, in order to stir them up and make them think. She was making a point to demonstrate an example of integration in their town. Their response to us was usually one of shock.

The Bodines were absolutely wonderful people. I really enjoyed them – they were like family to me. They didn't have children of their own, so they helped to make summer school an enjoyable experience.

***

My major at Hampton was Early Childhood Education and my minor was Elementary Education, so I had to practice teach in both. On campus there was a nursery school and kindergarten and there was an elementary school just off campus. I did practice teaching in all three.

When I practice taught in the elementary school, one of my responsibilities was to create a document that could be used by young children to learn about the history of the area around Hampton, history significant for the nation. Pocahontas and her Powhatan tribe were from the same region. Of great importance, the first slave ships landed in that same area. There was no book at the time for elementary-age children, so my assignment was to create a book for them about the history of the local area. I wish I had kept that book that I created, but, unfortunately, I didn't.

I was a sophomore at Hampton in 1954 when the Supreme Court ruled in *Brown v. Board*, the decision that declared segregated schools were unlawful. In fact, I remember the day the court made the decision. I was with a group of friends on the lawn, in front of Virginia Hall, near the water. It was a beautiful setting, and sometimes we would sit there, collect oyster shells, and just enjoy the sea breezes. But I remember that day the announcement was made, those of us from Southern states were all kind of in shock. We were all thinking, "Wow, never thought this would happen!"

This was the first law to pass that impacted anything significant in terms of beginning to overturn Jim Crow laws. Before then it had been business as usual. So, when we heard the news on May 17, 1954, we weren't really sure what would happen next, or what impact this would have. Our attitude in response to the news was: "Wait and see." The law said that integration would take place as soon as possible, "with all deliberate speed." We knew that meant it was going to take a long time.

***

As I neared graduation, Professor Powell, head of the Early Childhood Education department, encouraged me to accept an internship at Wellesley College. But I, in my youthful "wisdom," decided I'd had enough with school and wanted to work. I was anxious to get out and teach. The Wellesley internship, I realized in my later years, was an opportunity that could have been a good experience for me, had I chosen to go.

I graduated from Hampton in May 1956. My experience there was fantastic. When my family (mother, aunt, and two brothers) drove to Virginia to attend my graduation ceremony, they used something called the "Green Book." It was formatted by someone whose last name was Green (not a relative), and it identified places where Black people could stay overnight and restaurants they could go to when traveling.

People may not realize how important the Green Book was and how necessary it was, for Black people, when traveling by car in the South. It was a necessity because Jim Crow laws meant we couldn't stay in hotels in the South. When you were on a long motor trip, overnight accommodations were necessary.

Jim Crow was an ongoing consideration in everything that we did. I can remember vividly when we left Hampton after my graduation, we reached Charleston, West Virginia at dusk. We were on our way to visit New York, and then we were going to Wilberforce, Ohio, before returning home to Little Rock. When we reached Charleston that evening, I remember my aunt stopping the car and asking a Black gentleman where Mrs. So-and-So's house was. He directed us there, and we spent the night at this lady's house. She was someone listed in the Green Book as providing accommodations for Black people.

Again, my mother and aunt never discussed why or how we did things, they just did what had to be done. Of course, when we arrived in New York City, we could stay in a hotel because we were in a northern state where the Jim Crow laws did not apply. In fact, we stayed in the famous Hotel Theresa in Harlem. Fidel Castro and his entourage made a famous stay there some years later. As always, Mother and Auntie made sure that everything was in order.

After my graduation from Hampton, I had three teaching offers from Richmond, Virginia, Washington, DC, and Baltimore, Maryland. At the time Baltimore was one of the "hot spots" for kindergarten programs which were just beginning to take off in public school systems. Since my major was Early Childhood Education, I was excited by the opportunity to be part of that environment, so I accepted my first teaching job and began teaching kindergarten in the Baltimore City Public Schools.

SIX

KINDERGARTEN TEACHER

I have to laugh when I think about how I taught kindergarten before Velcro was invented! One year, I had thirty-two children in the morning and thirty-nine in the afternoon. In winter, half the time was spent getting them out of the winter gear, and then back into it before they went home! I remember one student who never learned to put on his coat and would get the sleeves crisscrossed. We would go through the lesson on how to put on a coat, and I would put his coat on the floor to get him to put his arms in the sleeves, but it didn't work, so I would have to dress him every day in winter. There were always many children who couldn't tie their shoes, couldn't button their coats, and couldn't zip up—and at that time there were no such things as "teacher aides"! Fortunately, I usually found one mature child in the class who could help me "dress" the others.

One year, when I was teaching kindergarten in Baltimore, it was the year that Alan Shepard became the first astronaut in space! I was able to get the principal to allow my class to watch the launch on the school's one TV. Nobody had ever seen anything like that before! It was important for me to research the topic, in order to interpret the experience to my kindergarteners. The goal of the space mission was to put an astronaut into orbit around the Earth, and I had to learn what "orbit" meant (that was not in the vocabulary yet). When I explained "orbit" to my kindergarten students, I would have one person stand still (the Earth) and the other child would go around and around as the spaceship.

We wrote an "experience story" about this, as we always did in my kindergarten classes, following a special event. One student took the story home. I saw that student about twenty years ago, and she told me she had kept that story all these years! It was a truly memorable experience for me and my students.

As a teacher, I wanted to provide experiences for my young learners that would help them to develop a love of learning. I believed kindergarten was the time to focus on "reading readiness" rather than formal reading lessons (twenty-five were at the "getting ready to read" stage, while only a few would actually have been ready to start formal reading lessons). We did exciting things like creating and presenting the *The Nutcracker* before the holidays with the students as the actors in the production.

Because there was usually a big "let down" after the Christmas holiday break, I would always try to create an interesting focus for the children. We would take an imaginary trip to Mexico in January. Although I could not speak Spanish, together we learned a song in Spanish, and how to count to ten in Spanish. I would have the students trace our route on the map from Baltimore to Mexico. The culmination of this unit was to translate our favorite story, *The Three Bears*, into Spanish. Goldilocks became "Conchita," and she visited the "casa" of the three bears. We would often perform our dramatizations for other classes, parents, and families.

Another favorite unit was about colors in the fall. As a class we would take a walk and look at the leaves. When we came back inside, I would ask the class about the colors they saw. One time I was conducting a demonstration lesson for teachers from other schools and used our "Fall Walk" as the focus. Of course, I asked my students about the leaf colors we saw on our walk. One very precocious student answered, "Purple!" I replied, "Purple is a very nice color, but let's think about the colors of the leaves."

It was important to me to encourage children and to help them have a positive feeling about learning. At no point did I want them to feel as though their answer was "wrong." I wanted them to feel curious and engaged. I think young learners are better served by providing enriching experiences, to learn by doing.

I still have an aversion to Halloween from my years as a kindergarten teacher. On Halloween the morning children would come in, and I would usually have a parent help me, but we would help them get on their costumes, then we would parade around the block. Following the "parade" we would come back to the classroom for our Halloween party. The costume removal and preparation for home would end just in time for me to grab a bite of lunch and prepare for the afternoon class. We would do the same thing—in and out of the costumes, parade around the block, come back and have a party.

The children of course were always so excited, so it was necessary to conjure up the same amount of enthusiasm for the afternoon as you did for the morning, even though you were ready to collapse. When my son was little, when I arrived home, we did Halloween with him. It was exhausting! Fortunately, I was young, with lots of energy. Now, when I see four and five-year-olds, I remember why I don't do it anymore! But I truly enjoyed it; I was committed to the children.

My mother used to come to visit in the summer after she completed her teaching responsibilities in Little Rock. She would come and spend a couple of weeks with us, and she would always come at the time when I was completing the attendance report for the year, because our schools closed a little later in Baltimore. This was the pre-computer era. She used to say, "I don't know how you do it," referring to the annual attendance wrap-up for seventy (or more) children. You knew what you had to do, and whatever it took you just did it. I can remember those forms with the percentage of absences and all the required calculation. I really had to use my brain!

***

Several years ago, I was shopping in Nordstrom's. When I finished making my purchase, a lady came up to me and said, "Aren't you a teacher?" I said, "Well, I was many years ago in Baltimore City." She named several schools, and I said, "No, I didn't teach there, but my very first school after I finished college was School #120 on Pennsylvania Avenue."

She looked at me and said, "I knew it! You are Miss Green! I would recognize you anywhere. You were my kindergarten teacher." It turned out she was in my first kindergarten class after I finished college. She said, "You know as the years pass, you forget the bad ones, but you always remember the good ones, and I will always remember being in your class."

For somebody to have good memories of school and to help instill the desire of a young person to learn—that's why you teach. It was really a moving experience for me, and I was just stunned by it. I felt like I had won an Oscar! To make a positive impression on a kindergartener is important because that tends to stick with children throughout their lives. What made it so meaningful was that first year of teaching, I wasn't sure if I had deterred the students from ever going to school again! But evidently something worked.

I did not remember her, but I would never let her know that and since it was over fifty years ago, I guess that can be excused. But at least there was one student who felt that that year was worthwhile. The goal of teaching is to help people become better citizens, but you rarely get the chance to know if you were successful or not.

That experience reminded me of things I have heard people say about being in my mother's first-grade class at Stephens. There are still people in Little Rock who talk about what a wonderful experience it was and how they enjoyed being in her class. She knew how to create a calm learning environment where students felt safe and secure. She was very good at classroom management!

SEVEN

CENTRAL HIGH CRISIS

In the fall of 1957, when I was starting my second year as a kindergarten teacher in Baltimore, my brother Ernest was about to begin his senior year of high school.

After the 1954 *Brown v. Board* Supreme Court decision school systems were encouraged to integrate as soon as possible. But, of course, that meant many different things to many different people and individuals.

It was the Little Rock School Board that decided that they would integrate because school systems were under pressure to do something, so they began with the high school. Students were identified at Horace Mann High School (newly opened when Dunbar became a middle school), who would be eligible, based on deportment, academic grades, and other proof of achievement.

At first, a fairly large number of students were identified to be the first students to integrate Little Rock Central High School. However, as time passed, and decisions were made, only nine students chose to do so. My brother, Ernest, was one of the nine, and was the only senior in the group.

When Ernest was identified as one of the people who could transfer to Little Rock Central High School, he mentioned it to my mother and my aunt. My mother said, "Well, if this is what you want to do, we'll support you." They did not make a big thing of it. Neither he nor my mother ever talked about the criteria for being able to go, but he was given the opportunity, and he chose to accept it.

Ernest wanted to transfer because Central was clearly the better facility, with better materials and a greater variety of classes. We often laugh, because anybody—even a person who could not see—could understand that a building three times the size of Dunbar or Horace Mann would have three times as much going on.

When Ernest became one of the nine to integrate Central, it was astounding to me. It was just so unthinkable based on my experience growing up in Little Rock. My internal response was, "I never thought I would live to see the day." I am sure my mother and aunt thought the same.

My brother talks about the summer before he entered Central, when he was working at a country club in Little Rock. During the summer, he had become friendly with one of the White boys whose parents were members of the country club. When Ernest's name appeared in the newspaper as one of the nine students going to Central, the boy came up to Ernest and said, "I am just shocked. I thought you were a nice person."

The implied second half of that statement was unsaid, but it was, "I thought you were a nice person [who knew your place]." The unsaid part expressed the sentiment: "How could you think you were good enough to come to my school?" Ernest said at that point he figured if people were getting that upset about him going to Central, there must be something great there that he needed to take advantage of and that inspired him even more.

That story exemplifies the attitude that many White people had, when they realized that Ernest and the others had the "audacity" to want to integrate Central High School. It shows how deeply some people did not want to change anything. Many White children growing up in the South had been trained to feel people who did not look like them were not worthy to associate with them. That's the heart of it. The attitude was as long as they "stay in their place" everybody's happy.

Unfortunately, that's the basis of a lot of the attitudes we see today as well. The assumption based on ignorance is that "those people" (meaning Black people) are never going to amount to anything, so why waste time and money on them? These kinds of attitudes and ideas were based on things that happened for hundreds and hundreds of years and are still pervasive. It's tragic when you think about it. Each time some White people felt their status quo was being confronted, they rebelled instead of trying to understand the rationale and seeing how people could work together.

The school board informed the nine Black students that they would only be able to attend academic classes and would not be allowed to join clubs or take part in any extracurricular activities at Central. Ernest had played saxophone in the band at Dunbar and Horace Mann. But it was made very clear to the Nine that they would not participate in any activities like that at Central. They could forget about pursuing interests like that.

Fortunately, students at Dunbar and Horace Mann were extremely close. Ernest's friends at Horace Mann sustained him that year. When he was shut out of activities at Central, they involved him in all their social activities. He remains friends with many of them. They believed in and supported him that year.

***

On September 4, 1957, the first day the Nine were supposed to begin classes at Central High School, an angry White mob surrounded the school, and the Arkansas National Guard blocked the students from entering the building. They were told immediately to leave for their safety because the rioters would possibly harm the students. The threat of violence was very real.

I will never forget that day. That morning, my principal, Mrs. Wright, came in my classroom and said, "Treopia! Did you hear about the rioting in Little Rock?" Her words shocked me. I had no idea what she was talking about. I couldn't imagine that happening in my hometown because I had never experienced Little Rock as a violent place. That evening after work I turned on the television and saw the rioting outside of Central. I was stunned by the level of anger and hostility aimed at my brother and the other students.

I still remember, when I was home the weekend before Ernest was to begin at Central, seeing the headlines in the *Arkansas Gazette* newspaper. One of the articles described a meeting between Arkansas Governor Faubus and Governor Coleman of Mississippi. I will always believe that Governor Faubus's actions, that Monday, to command the Arkansas National Guard to prevent the students from entering Central High School—going against what had been mandated by the Supreme Court and planned for by the Little Rock School Board—were partially a result of that meeting with the Mississippi governor.

People in Little Rock who live near Central still talk about the fact that there were a lot of out-of-state cars parked in the neighborhood that first day of classes. Even though there was strict segregation in accordance with Jim Crow laws, Little Rock was not a hostile place. In comparison, Mississippi was much more hostile towards Black people at that time. That's why I think when that meeting was held the weekend before school was to start, when Faubus met with the Mississippi governor, he was pressured by Coleman not to "let down" the other southern governors who were staunch segregationists.

Faubus was, I think, easily persuaded. The change about the National Guard's mission was made just like that. The decision to prevent the students from entering was a complete reversal, a "180," for Governor Faubus. I remember, when that happened, my mother said, "And to think I voted for him in the last election." No one expected him to do that. This is what I believe really angered President Eisenhower. He was not going to let some upstart governor go against what had been ruled by the Supreme Court to take place. What kind of precedent would that have set?

After my shock at seeing the violent rioting outside of Central High School on television, I immediately called home that evening, and my mother's words, which she said every time I called that year, were, "Treopia, we are just fine. Don't worry about us. You have your kindergarten children to be concerned about. We are okay."

She said these soothing words, even as I saw the mobs going berserk outside of Central. I would call home every night that year, however I still don't know the full extent of the negative things my family lived through because my mother never talked about that to me.

After the first day, the decision was made to pull the Nine out. It was too dangerous for them to try to go to school. They went to Mrs. Daisy Bates' house and were tutored there every day. I remember, on Ernest's birthday, September 22, my mother called me to say that she had just received a telegram from President Eisenhower, as did the other eight parents. President Eisenhower announced that he was sending troops to make sure the students would get into school safely. He sent one thousand army paratroopers to Little Rock, and they set up camp with tents on the Central High grounds.

Daisy Bates' home was a hub for the Little Rock Nine. In addition to publishing the Black newspaper, the *Arkansas State Press*, with her husband, L.C. Bates, she was also president of the Arkansas chapter of the NAACP. When it became official that the students would integrate Central, she assumed the responsibility of leadership for that transition. It would have been improper for any of the parents to provide that leadership because their responsibility was to keep things as calm as possible at home and support their children. Because of her position and interest, Daisy Bates was the best person for this role. Assuming this role, however, put her and her husband at even greater risk for violence. The Bates' home was vandalized multiple times and the target of a firebomb.

The next morning, September 23, after the soldiers' arrival, the students met at Daisy Bates' house, where they were picked up in two cars with a jeep in front with machine guns and a jeep behind with machine guns. My brother's comment was, "I think we will get in school today."

This was the only integration case in which troops were used. After President Eisenhower deployed the troops, other places, even though it was not smooth, did not require that kind of intervention. It is just almost unbelievable when you think of it—one thousand troops to escort nine high school students.

President Eisenhower was probably perturbed by Governor Faubus not obeying the Supreme Court decision. I believe that he was more disturbed about that than he was about integrating Central

High. But whatever his rationale, it worked out to support Ernest and the other eight. When they arrived at school, each of them had a personal guard who would go with them to class and stand outside the classroom door.

However, Ernest said when they went to gym class, they didn't have that protection. There was one time when he and the two other Black boys were showering after gym class, and when they stepped out of the shower, someone had put broken glass right in front of the door, so they stepped on broken glass. Sometimes someone would flip a switch on them, in the shower, to make the water go all cold, or all hot.

My family received threatening phone calls at the house all during that year. My brother Scott was fourteen at the time, and he answered the phone many times when calls like that came in. Although he never shared the details with me, I know horrible things were said, and it pains me to think about the effect that had on him at his age.

***

During the crisis that fall, my family had a distraction since my wedding was set to take place in December. As President Eisenhower was sending the National Guard to escort Ernest and the others to school for their protection, at the same time my mother was planning my wedding and creating my wedding dress. It was a beautiful dress, embroidered with hundreds of pearls. With her exquisite taste and execution, she embraced the finer points of dressmaking. I felt guilty about that later—how could I have imposed on her with everything that was going on that year?

But, when I expressed that to her friends years later, they told me that having that distraction was the best thing that could have happened because it gave her a chance to focus on something else and take her mind off the Central High fiasco. Her friends convinced me of this because I felt so guilty but knowing her that makes sense. Sewing was her hobby, and she loved to do embroidery and smocking—the more challenging the garment, the more she enjoyed making it. So, the wedding gown was "right up her alley"!

My wedding was on December 22, 1957, the Sunday before Christmas. Because of our many family friends and acquaintances, I sent out four hundred wedding invitations! It was held at my church, Bethel AME, immediately after service. The weather was unseasonably warm. In fact, I just wore a thin shawl over my shoulders; I didn't have to wear a winter coat.

My brothers, Ernest and Scott, served as ushers and my grandfather gave me away. Following the ceremony, the reception was held at home like all social events. Most people were coming from church, and the reception lasted about three hours. Daisy Bates and her husband, L.C., were friends of our family, so they were there. The following week my bridal picture was in the *Arkansas State Press*, the newspaper they published.

The reception was catered by someone with whom my father had worked. She gave this to me as a wedding gift. My mother not only made my dress, but also my two bridesmaids' dresses, and the tablecloth. The bridesmaids' dresses were green taffeta, and they carried red and white bouquets—Christmas colors. Our dining room was beautifully decorated. I was in the living room with my husband greeting guests and receiving gifts. I wore beautiful white satin high heel shoes, and I remember how much my feet were hurting!

When it came time to do the thank-you notes, my mother insisted that I handwrite them. She was not going to have any printed notes. Her philosophy was, if people thought enough about you to give you a gift, then the least you could do is handwrite a note. So, I handwrote almost four hundred thank-you notes. I think it was spring before I was finished! But I can truly appreciate her philosophy.

***

After Christmas, in late winter, early spring, I learned the situation had gotten particularly bad for Ernest. I remember the day well when I called home and Ernest told me about his physics teacher. Ernest had prepared his project for the class and taken it to school and put it in his locker. When he went to his locker after lunch, someone had broken into his locker and destroyed his work. That gave his physics teacher an excuse to give him a failing grade.

Things had continued to get rougher, so my mother asked him if he wanted to come to Baltimore to stay with me and my husband and finish his school year there. But Ernest's decision was no. Even though at that point he and the other students were dealing with threats and attempted physical violence at times, and destruction of their schoolwork. In fact, he said, "I accepted this responsibility, and I expect to see it through." Ernest also said the death of Emmett Till, a young teenage boy who was lynched in 1955 while visiting relatives in Mississippi, inspired him to stay committed and make it through that year.

Fortunately, there was an instructor at the University of Arkansas Medical School, Dr. Wixom, who took an interest in Ernest. He tutored him every Saturday at his home. With Dr. Wixom's support, Ernest passed physics. When I came home for a visit in the summer of 1958, after Ernest had successfully completed his year and graduated from Central High School, I met Dr. Wixom and his wife, who invited me to their home for lunch.

My mother was the kind of person who didn't "worry," however, it's an indication of how bad things were that she was considering how to get Ernest out of Little Rock to finish his high school education elsewhere, if that's what he had wanted to do.

People asked my mother several times through the years, "How did you cope when Ernest was going to Central with everything going on?" My mother's reply was "I'm a person of faith."

Mother had a very strong faith, but she was not a Bible-toting person who would tell people what to do. She had an inner faith and that gave her the strength that she had. As a parent she must have had concern every day, but she didn't let it bother her, she just did what she could. She would tell me, "If you have an issue, you analyze it, do what you can about it, and then leave it alone." That's how she lived.

***

Ernest completed his mission and graduated from Central in May 1958.

The Reverend Dr. Martin Luther King, Jr. attended Ernest's graduation. He was the commencement speaker at what was then Arkansas AM&N (an HBCU) and is now the University of Arkansas at Pine Bluff. Dr. King heard about Ernest's graduation, so he called Daisy Bates and asked if he could come. He had not become as famous yet as he ultimately became. Had it been so, he would not have been able to be there.

There is a photo that shows Dr. King getting in the car with my mother. After Dr. King called Mrs. Bates, she called my mother and told her that Dr. King wanted to come. So, he came to our house, and went to the graduation with my family. In the guestbook for Ernest's graduation, is Dr. King's name and address, with a graduation gift to Ernest of $15, about $150 in today's currency.

The day before Ernest was to graduate, the principal called and asked if he wanted his diploma mailed to him, because they had received a threat that if Ernest walked across the stage he would be shot. Ernest's response was, "I did not go through this year not to let my family see me receive my diploma, so I am going to participate in the graduation ceremonies."

Although the possibility of violence was real, he knew what his goal was. His goal was to receive the diploma at graduation. I've often heard him describe graduation: when the other students walked across the stage, to receive their diplomas, there was loud applause and cheering, but when he walked across, there was an eerie silence.

I had to stay in Baltimore during Ernest's graduation. I was finishing the year with my kindergarteners, a morning class of thirty-two students and an afternoon class of thirty-nine students. In those days, teachers were not excused from teaching, unless you were seriously ill. I didn't even think about going to the graduation because I knew I could not leave my students.

However, if I had known then what I know now, I would have made every effort to be there. But I celebrated with him from a distance. There is a photo of Ernest standing with our mother, calling me on the phone and telling me, "I made it." I was glad to receive the information that everything went well, but it was not something our family carried on about.

***

Following Ernest's graduation from Central, the Hotel and Restaurant Workers Union Local 6 in New York City invited the nine students and Daisy Bates to New York. I was invited to join them, and it was an experience I will never forget. We met the actress Lena Horne, who was also active in civil rights work, and were guests at her musical, *Jamaica*, on Broadway. She was very complimentary of the achievements of the Little Rock Nine.

We also met with Governor Averell Harriman in his suite at the Waldorf Astoria. We had lunch at the United Nations and met Ralph Bunche, the first African American to be awarded the Nobel Peace Prize. That was when I first became aware of paparazzi, because while we were trying to eat lunch, they were all on tables taking pictures. I thought to myself, "How rude!" I had to become accustomed to that, though, whenever I was with Ernest.

Ernest and mother were informed, by Michigan State University, that Ernest would receive the offer of a full four-year scholarship with all expenses paid. There was no question about whether he would accept it. Ernest didn't find out until twenty years later who had given him the full scholarship to Michigan State University.

He was a speaker at MSU graduation several years ago and I went with him because I had never been to Michigan State. We were having breakfast at the home of the current MSU president, and he asked Ernest, "Do you know who provided the four year all-expense paid scholarship to Michigan State?" Because it was given to him anonymously. He said no, and for the first time, we were told that it was the president of Michigan State, President Hannah, in 1958. We had not known that before then. Ernest has continued to support MSU in many ways, including the establishment of a scholarship in the Department of Social Work.

Bottom line: there are more good people in the world than there are evil people.

***

Later when Ernest would go back to Little Rock to attend Central class reunions, he would chuckle because everyone there was so happy to see him and told him that they were so pleased they had been in the class with him. They have also told him that they knew he would be successful. Everybody was his friend, and nobody was against him. Ernest just laughed about this because when he was a student that could not have been farther from the truth. We all had a good laugh when we heard him tell this.

Many times, people don't realize, when they're participating in negative activities, the impact that it can have, and what it can do to people. Over the years they just kind of brush it off as if it was inconsequential; almost like they don't want to take responsibility for their actions. I think some would even deny that it took place.

When Ernest went to his last reunion, he took as his guest, the first Black candidate for mayor of Little Rock. The campaign happened to be going on at the same time as Ernest's class reunion, so he took him as his guest, and introduced him to people. One of the Central High alums wrote a campaign donation check for $500 on the spot. I guess that was a way of saying "I'm sorry" to Ernest.

It's really strange how life evolves. I have a feeling there are quite a few who wish they had acted differently.

***

An interesting follow up is that several years ago the city of Abilene, Kansas celebrated the 100th birthday of President Dwight

Eisenhower, and Ernest was invited to be on the panel. At the time, Orval Faubus, the former governor of Arkansas, was also there. He made the statement that Ernest's success after Central was due to him, meaning Faubus.

When Ernest told me that, we laughed because it's just so absurd and ridiculous that you can't even take it seriously. Ernest didn't even bother to respond to such a statement. You just shake your head and move on.

One of the things that our parents instilled in us was not to lower ourselves by engaging with others who were being ignorant or foolish. You don't fall to those depths to even confront that type of horrific behavior.

***

Once when Ernest was giving a speech, a student in the audience asked, "Were you going to Central to make history?" And Ernest said, "No, I was going to get an education."

I think it's important for young people to realize history is made long after something happens. When we look back on events, we see how the choices people make are what creates history, but at the time people are not thinking of it in those terms. They are acting in the here and now and asking themselves, "What is the correct thing to do in this moment?"

We owe a lot of that to our mother, who firmly believed that "if this is what you're committed to, we will support you." If it's something you committed to do, then you do it because you believe it is the right thing to do.

EIGHT

THE LOST YEAR

After Ernest's graduation, the following school year, 1958-59, became known as the "Lost Year" in Little Rock because Governor Faubus closed all the city's high schools to try to further block desegregation. He was determined that no other Black students would graduate and do what Ernest had accomplished.

This act caused a lot of harm and disrupted the education of all high school students in Little Rock, including my brother Scott. It spurred the development of private academies that were created for White students. But for Black students that was not an option, and it's estimated that 50% were not able to find alternative options for their education that year.

My mother desperately wanted to keep Scott close to home and tried to place him in eight different school districts, but because she was teaching, the logistics of getting him to another district just wouldn't work. She decided in October 1958 the only alternative she had for him would be to go to Oakland, California to stay with my father's sisters, whom he had never met, and attend school there for his sophomore year. It must have been a very hurtful decision for my mother to have to send him away.

That was a very difficult year for Scott. After all he and my family went through during the desegregation crisis, Scott had to move a thousand miles away just to continue his high school education. This was also only a few years after our father had passed, when Scott was ten years old.

A few years ago, he and I started talking almost every Sunday on the phone, and it was only recently that he told me about his experiences during the Lost Year. In one of our conversations, Scott mentioned that he asked my mother if she would think about getting married again because he really missed having a father. I think he suffered the most when my father passed away because he was so young.

In the summer of 1959 federal courts declared the school closures unconstitutional, and schools reopened that fall. Scott returned to Little Rock, but he did not go back to high school. Instead of completing high school, Scott joined the Air Force and married a girl from Little Rock.

Scott and his bride moved to North Dakota where he was stationed with the Air Force. He said one day his commanding officer told him with almost no notice that he was going to take his GED® test the next morning. When he took the test, he aced it. He said it was easy for him—nothing to it!

Ernest and I always agreed Scott was the smartest of the three of us. But one of the things Scott expressed to me during our Sunday phone visits was that he felt Mother was disappointed that he didn't go to college. His academic growth was blocked due to the school closure and the effect that had on him.

Scott never pursued college, but I think he would have been a formidable force had he gone that route. Unfortunately, you really need that kind of credential to do a lot of things. I am convinced that the direction Scott's life took was a direct result of the fallout after the '57 Central desegregation crisis.

Scott and his wife had a son, Scott Jr., but divorced soon after he was born. Scott moved to New York City where he joined the Recruitment and Training Program (RTP). Ernest was Executive Director of the program, which was sponsored by A. Phillip Randolph and Bayard Rustin, both civil rights icons.

The goal of the program was to increase the number of minority workers in construction trades. Scott later became the first Black union member of the Sheet Metal Workers Local 28 in New York City. When someone asked him why he chose that trade, he said when he learned that union had no Black members, he was curious to find out why. He fought discrimination and brought more Black sheet metal workers into the union.

Like my mother and aunt before him, Scott was part of a lawsuit for civil rights. The lawsuit was brought against the union because of its discriminatory practices providing smaller pensions and fewer work opportunities for minority workers. The suit dragged on for decades and was finally settled in 2015. The plaintiffs received a minimal cash award for unpaid back wages, but at least they won the suit. If something was unfair, Scott was the type of person who would challenge it. I think all of us inherited that quality from our mother.

Professor John A. Kirk details the links between the lawsuits for teachers' salary equalization, like the one in Little Rock that my mother and aunt were part of in the 1940s, and the *Brown v. Board of Education* ruling to desegregate public schools, which led to Ernest being one of the nine students who desegregated Central High School. The attitude in our family was to pursue legal means in the struggle for equality. We never talked about it overtly, but the goal was to bring about change. It is always important to pursue a situation lawfully, in order to protect the rights to which all citizens are entitled by the Constitution.

As a sheet metal worker, Scott helped to build the World Trade Center and worked on several skyscrapers in New York City. Scott was proud of his work in New York, but, like my mother, he never talked about his accomplishments.

I remember the time Scott called me, many years ago, because he was upset about a situation at one of his construction jobs. Scott and three other Black sheet metal workers were hired to work on a high-rise building, but he said the minute they showed up for work that morning, they were fired. Scott said the foreman didn't even have the decency to give them the checks they were due but told them where they could go and pick them up. He said they were immediately replaced with White workers.

Scott felt strongly that he and his colleagues were hired because of the law that stipulated a certain tax break for hiring people of color. Scott felt the owner was exploiting a loophole in the law— just because minorities were hired, it was not mandatory to keep them. They were hired, fired, and replaced. Scott was furious about the experience when he called me, and felt it was a terrible injustice that they would operate in such a way.

Within our family, my brother Scott had a more confrontational attitude than either Ernest or I. I really think Scott perhaps didn't acquire the more diplomatic approach because of what he had to endure during the Central High crisis and afterward during the Lost Year. Scott was on the outside watching the things that were happening to his older brother, and I think he felt what Ernest was enduring was just unforgivable, and he felt more action should have been taken. But, in fact, that would not have helped at all.

I often think had Scott been the one in Ernest's position, the outcomes would not have been as good. Ernest's personality was more conducive to enduring what he had to go through without lashing out to defend himself. Ernest had an extraordinary amount of self-control and still does. However, with his participation in the labor lawsuit, Scott pursued things in a way that he knew the family would approve of through legal recourse. Although it can take more time and effort, pursuing legal means of change can ultimately lead to more successful outcomes.

Scott loved living in New York. He married again there, and eventually had another son, Shomari Green. After his marriage dissolved, he moved to Harlem, where he resided in the same apartment, a five-story "walk-up," for twenty years. During this time, he would travel to Brazil, with a friend, and spend most winters. There, he became an avid soccer fan, calling it "the real football." In summers, he loved to swim, and always enjoyed the New York beaches. Each year, on my birthday, he would come to Baltimore on the afternoon train, celebrate the day, and leave on the last train to New York. He never spent the night because it was "too quiet" here.

***

My brother Scott contracted COVID-19 in the spring of 2020. After spending a couple weeks at a hospital, he was moved to a Rehabilitation Center. I called Scott at the Rehab Center, around 3:15 in the afternoon on Easter Sunday. We talked for a couple minutes, and I said I would call again later. I called about 7:15 that evening, not wanting to wait too late. This time he sounded extremely weak. He explained that he was wearing a mask, and tubes had been placed in his body. After a few seconds, I told him that he should not talk any more, because he needed to rest, and I would call tomorrow. At 11:00 that night, the nurse called, saying, "Scott has passed away."

Every day, since early 2020, the coronavirus victim numbers increase. As of this writing, more than 980,000 lives have been claimed in the United States. On Easter Sunday, April 12, 2020, my brother, Scott Green, became one of those numbers. He died that day, alone (no visitors allowed), in New York City.

We have a family burial plot at a cemetery in Little Rock that I always visit when I go home. My mother, father, grandfather, grandmother, aunt, uncle, and my great-grandparents on my mother's side are all buried there. When a blind man, who was a member of our church, passed and did not have a burial place, my mother made sure he was buried in our family plot. We were hoping to have Scott buried there as well, but his remains are still in New York and will probably stay there.

After Scott passed, we struggled to locate a funeral home in the New York area to which his body could be released. They were all over capacity, so we reluctantly fell to the mercy of the New York City mortuary to bury him in the public burial grounds – Hart Island. This was a heart-breaking experience. However, we were blessed to connect with wonderful, understanding people, and we continue to communicate to this day. A bright light in this journey is the relationship that has developed with the exciting and meaningful Hart Island Project.

Scott was one of the thousands of people who died during the COVID-19 outbreak in New York in the beginning of 2020. Many of them were buried on Hart Island. I'm involved in the Hart Island Project, working with a group that is trying to work with elected officials to turn Hart Island into a National Cemetery because there are so many people buried there who died in the early days of the global pandemic. We must never forget that each one is not just a number but a missing part of a grieving family.

NINE

FAMILY GROWTH AND CHANGE

My son, Todd, was born in 1964. Actually, his due date was December 28, 1963. Ernest and his wife at the time came down to Baltimore from New York to be there for the baby's birth. My mother was also staying with me for the birth. I didn't know what the baby's sex would be, so I decorated the nursery in pink, yellow, and blue. Ernest's son, Adam, who was six months old, christened the crib in the nursery. I was extremely pregnant, and I remember on New Year's Eve everyone was sitting around looking at me, like, "When is this baby going to be born?"

Well, my son Todd decided he wasn't going anywhere. Ernest and his family had to return home to New York on the first of January, but my mother was able to stay and be there for his birth on January 2. He was a healthy baby at 7lbs 2.5 oz. and 21 inches long. According to his height and weight at birth, it was predicted he would be 6 feet tall—which he is almost.

Todd was four months old when I went back to work. I hadn't planned to go back that soon, but a principal that I knew was opening a new school, Mary Rodman Elementary School, and she asked me to be the kindergarten teacher. I agreed to do that, and Todd's aunt, his father's sister, was able to take care of him during the day.

Todd and Adam are six months apart, and Scott's son, Scott Jr., was born just a few months before Adam, so my mother became a grandmother to three little boys within the span of about a year! She really enjoyed her role as a grandmother. Scott Jr. grew up in Little Rock, so my mother got to spend the most time with him, but she was very close to all her grandchildren, and they were very fond of her. Every summer she would fly to Baltimore and spend a lot of time with us. We would always go to New York to spend time as a family with Ernest and Scott.

From time to time we would ask my mother if she would like to move away from Little Rock and come stay with us, but she would always say, "I have my house, I have my friends, I am just fine." When my Aunt Treopia passed in 1959, she left her car to my mother, so my mother had to learn to drive late in life, and she did! She was very active in the community with various groups and her church.

My brothers and I have all lived in different places as adults. With the strength of my family, I think we all wanted to prove that we could do things independently. Even though there was a geographical distance between us, we stayed in touch frequently. I would dare say we are closer in terms of our relationships with each other than many people who live in the same place.

For closer support when I needed it, I learned to depend on neighbors, and I had many good friends who became like family. When Todd was little, we had neighbors who became very close friends, and that was important, especially for Todd since we didn't have family for him to spend time with on a daily basis. It goes back to the Golden Rule that I was raised by, "Do unto others as you would have them do unto you."

***

94

I began attending Johns Hopkins University the summer after my first year of teaching. It was conveniently located close to my home in Baltimore. I had saved up enough money to start courses there, and I initially just planned to do six hours above my bachelor's degree. But my mother said, very wisely, "That doesn't make sense. Once you start, you should just continue until you earn your master's." So, twice a week I took courses in the evening after teaching kindergarten and then in the summer I did several sessions.

My mother was visiting during the summer I finished my master's degree. Todd was still little, so Mother would help me with him while I studied, and she would use my portable sewing machine. One day when I came home from class, Mother had made a new bedspread and chair cover for my bedroom.

That was also the summer when Buzz Aldrin and Neil Armstrong landed on the moon. I remember because I was typing my final term paper on the typewriter while the excitement was happening on television. I graduated with my master's in Education in 1969. I recently received a lovely medallion from Johns Hopkins celebrating my fiftieth anniversary of having received my degree.

***

Around the time Todd was about to enter second grade, I changed from Baltimore City schools and began working in the Baltimore County schools. After starting my new job, I was impressed by the quality of the school system, so I persuaded Todd's father that we should move, so that Todd could attend school there. We bought a house in Baltimore County when Todd was in third grade.

We moved to an area that was at the time primarily Jewish. We were the second Black family on the block. You could always tell when Christmas came because only those two homes had Christmas decorations. There were very few other Black students at Todd's school, most of the students were Jewish. Todd's best friend growing up was a boy named Ira who lived across the street from us. We attended Ira's bar mitzvah and later his wedding. Todd spent a lot of time at Ira's house and was welcomed to take part in his family's Jewish holiday celebrations.

***

Our extended family today is multiracial with family members by marriage from several different ethnic backgrounds. It never mattered in our family what ethnicity one was as long as they cared about the person in our family. My parents never focused on race or color or ethnicity.

When Todd was in third grade, I asked him a question about his teacher trying to find out who she was. I asked him what she looked like—and he didn't know. I was not going to ask him outright about her race, so I didn't find out who she was until the first PTA meeting. I think she was White, but I don't really remember either. It just didn't matter to us – it was irrelevant and immaterial.

And this was a lesson passed on from my parents. We were taught not to base how we felt about someone on what race or ethnicity they were or how they looked, but whether they were a good person, a kind person, someone we enjoyed being around. If you're confident enough in who you are and what you're doing, you need to know the facts about racism, but it doesn't change what you think about people.

I think being raised with that kind of outlook is what gave us the ability and motivated us to move on and try new things.

Maintaining that kind of openness to people who may look different, enabled me to avoid making assumptions or developing stereotypes about people. It reinforced what I learned from my mother and father: You accept people, and you value all people.

I also firmly believe that no matter how much professional expertise one possesses, no matter what the level of professionalism, if you don't know how to get along with people, it goes for naught. A guiding belief in my life is respect for all people. I truly believe that everybody has something to offer. Nobody is beneath anybody else. When that is demonstrated, good things can happen.

***

When Ernest was head of the Recruitment and Training Program (RTP), the 1976 conference was held in New Orleans, to coincide with Mardi Gras. Ernest invited the entire family to attend the conference, and we decided to have a celebration of Mother's birthday, March 6. The celebration took place on Monday evening, March 2, following the closing dinner of the conference. Immediately after the speaker, Congressman Andrew Young, the hotel maître d' wheeled out a huge cake, and all seven hundred attendees sang "Happy Birthday." It was the first time the family had all been together to celebrate Mother's birthday since I graduated from high school! Many prominent civil rights and labor leaders attended the conference, including A. Philip Randolph and Bayard Rustin.

The following morning was Mardi Gras. We all got up early to go to the Zulu Parade and later, we attended the King Rex Parade and just had a good time. Mother was probably tired, but never said a word. The next morning, after Mardi Gras, we were all at breakfast together, as a family, in the hotel restaurant. Some people who knew us said they stopped to look because Mother seemed to almost have a halo around her—there was something very serene about how she looked surrounded by all her children and grandchildren.

After breakfast, we went to the airport together to catch our different flights home—Todd, his father, and I to Baltimore and my mother to Little Rock. That was the last time I saw my mother alive. She went home, and the next thing I knew she was gone.

Our family friend, Lucille McCall, was at the house when Mother returned from New Orleans. Upon returning home, my mother asked Lucille if she would run to the drugstore to get some aspirin. Lucille said that was really strange because my mother had never asked her to do that before. While Lucille was out, my mother passed.

My brothers, Ernest and Scott, were planning to visit Mother after they wrapped up the conference. They got there just as the ambulance was taking her body away. Her death certificate said she had a heart attack, so it was very sudden. When we arrived at our house in Baltimore, the phone was ringing, and it was Ernest. He said, "Don't unpack, you've got to come home, mother has passed."

One of my mother's friends said that Mother had done something unusual earlier that day. She called and told them what a wonderful time she had with her children and grandchildren in New Orleans. It was surprising because my mother was never effusive like that about anything.

Her funeral was held on her birthday, March 6, 1976, and it was beautiful. Art Porter, Sr. played for the funeral. Many of the people who had been at the conference in New Orleans, instead of returning home, came to Little Rock to attend my mother's funeral. We had to work with a hotel to reserve a couple hundred rooms for all the additional guests. My mother had traveled before to Ernest's work events and conferences, so many of his colleagues knew her well and were fond of her. Bayard Rustin, a close advisor of Dr. Martin Luther King, Jr. and leader in the civil rights movement, served as one of the pallbearers at her funeral.

After she passed, the three of us, Ernest, Scott, and I, were in the lawyer's office to settle her affairs, and the lawyer remarked that he'd never seen a family so supportive of each other and working together so easily. That's what she would have expected of us.

Lucille became like my surrogate mother after Mother's death. She is in her late nineties now but has been able to remain in her own home with the help of her family. Todd and I always stay with her when we visit Little Rock.

My mother's passing happened in a way that was memorable. It is quite extraordinary to me the way things happened. How many people are able to have their passing occur at the height of a beautiful experience in their lives? I felt very fortunate that we were able to praise her publicly and honor her before she passed.

TEN

TEACHING EXPERIENCES

Shortly after I started teaching at Mary Rodman Elementary School, when Todd was a baby, another new school opened in a more economically depressed area of Baltimore. The teaching supervisor asked me if I would take the kindergarten class at Stuart Hill Elementary, Baltimore City's first open space school. In open space schools there were no walls between classrooms. It was a new experience, and I accepted the challenge.

The architect of the school building design was someone from New Jersey, who had a grandiose idea about an open space school with an amphitheater. In addition, there was landscaping that included trees planted in front and gym equipment installed on the playground. The night before the school opened, the jungle gym was moved halfway into the street, and many of the bushes, that were part of the newly planted landscaping, were pulled up. Not an ideal start to the year!

My experience at this school was unique. Kindergarten was really taking off in the 1960s and '70s and with my background in early childhood education, Stuart Hill—the first and last open space school to be built in Baltimore—was the third new school which I helped open as a kindergarten teacher. The other kindergarten teacher, in the space next to me, was brand new, a recent college graduate, so I was a mentor to her. I also had a practice teaching student, Bill, from Towson State University.

A set of quadruplets enrolled in kindergarten: two boys, and two girls. They were divided between the two classes, two in each. However, they would find each other (no walls), and they would wrestle. We would see this ball with eight arms and eight legs, rolling around. That was how they played with each other.

In the afternoon when it was time to go home, Bill's job was to collect the quads. He was a tall, blond young man, and he was wonderful. He would have one under each arm, and would be holding hands with the other two. Then, he would take them to their mother who was waiting outside. Unfortunately, I was not able to have a conversation with their mother because I did not speak Spanish, and this was before there were many ESL programs with teachers in schools. Their father was in the Coast Guard, and I don't think he came home very much. The quads were cute, and could be really sweet kids, but boy they were a handful! By the end of the year the quads had learned to respond to English. I have always wondered what happened to them.

That school experience was the most unusual I had in my teaching career because of the completely open design of the building. Ideally that type of design would work, but students would need to have developed a lot of self-control for it to work well. Many very young children have not developed that ability yet. The school building design made it difficult for us to teach the students effectively. The principal there was great and did her best to boost teacher morale. She often organized activities where we could bond with each other. One winter the entire faculty went on a ski trip. We all needed the support.

***

In the 1960s when the civil rights movement was at the forefront, the labor movement was also becoming prominent. The teacher's union in Baltimore called a strike when I was teaching kindergarten. There were two of us kindergarten teachers at my school, Mary Rodman Elementary, and the other one was younger than I.

Teachers striking was something new for me and those of us who were of a different generation. I looked out my classroom window and saw the younger kindergarten teacher holding a sign with other teachers walking down the sidewalk. That was such a strange phenomenon to me because teaching was my passion, and I didn't relate it to other work areas, such as factories where I had heard of strikes. I stayed out of the fray and attended to my kindergarten class.

***

My mother had been a longtime member of a group called Church Women United. Founded in 1941, Church Women United was an integrated group with a mission to celebrate unity and diversity and work for peace. This kind of group was very unusual at the time, especially during the Jim Crow days.

My mother didn't talk about it a lot, but I knew she went to the meetings, and she was very dedicated to that group. My mother did more quiet work like that than I will probably ever know. She was a firm believer in doing what was right, but she never would have been one of the people to march or carry a placard or do anything demonstrative, that was not her style, and it was not my style either.

In 1968, following a meeting of Church Women United, my mother and I were talking on the phone and she said, "You know, I'm really concerned about Reverend King. I'm concerned about his discussion regarding the Vietnam War." Several months after that, Dr. Martin Luther King, Jr. was assassinated. My mother was a very perceptive person. She didn't talk a lot about things, but I recall that conversation.

***

During the late 1960s, things really began to change. In 1968 the singer James Brown came out with the song, "Say It Loud—I'm Black and I'm Proud." When I was growing up, to be labeled "Black," was a high-level insult. The acceptable terms before that time were "Negro" or "colored." At water fountains signs said "Colored" or "White." When the term "Black" came to be embraced, turning what used to be an insult on its head, it was rather shocking. I admit it took me some doing to even be able to use the term.

I can remember returning to my alma mater to attend a homecoming game at Hampton against Howard University. The marching band stopped in the middle of the field and did the Black power salute with their right fists raised in the air. Seeing that actually frightened me. When I was growing up nobody would have ever thought of doing that, so it was disconcerting to me. This type of social change and upheaval had not been part of my previous experience. The sense of instability and volatility felt scary to me.

***

After my memorable experience teaching the quads in the open space school, I took on a new challenge as assistant director of

Baltimore's Model Early Childhood Learning Program. It was a pre-kindergarten program for three and four-year-olds and was the first of its kind to involve "hierarchical learning objectives."

There were only four of us in leadership positions, and it was an incredibly labor-intensive process. At the beginning of the program, I remember we were sitting on the floor of one of the superintendent's offices, and the requirement was for us to construct the entire curriculum. After deciding what the curriculum areas would be (color, form, etc.), we had to determine the hierarchy of learning objectives for each and then develop ten or twelve objectives, and identify skills for each, in order of difficulty.

For each of the skills that we developed, we created a manipulative task to match the objective. We created a starting point task and the completion of the skill task and the method of documentation. There were no computers, so this was all by hand. Each child in each class in each of the three schools had a sheet for each area and if there were twelve objectives in color, there were twelve boxes on the sheet, and a diagonal line in each. The top of the diagonal indicated the date the child started the task, and the bottom part indicated the date the child completed the task.

It was complicated, but the process was extraordinary, because at any given time you could identify exactly where a child was on any area on a specific day. The teachers had to keep records for each child for each day, which meant they were in school until six or seven o'clock at night compiling all this data.

It was the beginning of individualized learning because the parents and teachers could know exactly what each child was learning or what they were struggling with. The teacher could tell you that the child had begun to identify colors and then you come back the next week and the child could identify five colors. It was really fascinating, and it was a lot of work!

***

The director of the Baltimore County Title I program visited one of my classes at one of the schools I supervised for the Model Early Childhood Learning Program one day and said, "I would love to have you work in Baltimore County." I was intrigued by the offer and decided to make the change to the Baltimore County school system.

Working in Title I schools was a different scope for me. In general, the county schools were in more affluent areas, but since I worked in schools with Title I funding, the areas were poorer. Title I is a federal education program that provides extra funds to schools with the highest numbers of students experiencing poverty.

Many of the schools that were in Title I in Baltimore County were in all-White areas. There was one school in which there were no children of color and no teachers of color, and the only person of color was the school custodian. I started as a Title I resource teacher and then was appointed the first parent coordinator.

The Title I mandatory parent involvement programs have evolved into family engagement programs in schools today. In the 1970s, parent involvement was something completely new for schools, and here I was the only person of color and in charge of the parent involvement. It was an interesting experience, but a very positive experience.

Once when I was working with parents at one of my Title I schools, I overheard a White parent see me and say to another White parent, "Oh, that's the nice Black lady that comes in." I took that as a real compliment.

Parent involvement in the schools was a mandate, but it was a challenge to implement. I remember one principal who said to me, "I will not have parent programs in my school." And I said, "OK," but as I said it, I knew I was thinking of some way that I could get it done.

I saw my opening when he started a new reading program in the library. I was talking to him and said, "You know, the librarian is working so hard with that—maybe a parent could help her?" There were a couple of parents who would come up to the school. I said, "Why don't I ask Mrs. Jones if she would like to help?" So, that parent started and then we got a couple more and within about a month I said to the parents, "Why don't we get together and talk about the parent program?"

At the time having parents do work in the schools, more than just being on the PTA and baking cookies and cakes, was not something that had been done before, especially not in poorer areas. The Title I regulations required parent advisory councils in every Title I school. The president of the parent advisory council had to sign off on the school budget. That was the federal law. But there were some principals who were adamant about not wanting parents to come in to help run their school.

So, it was a bit of a power struggle.

I can remember that one principal banging on the desk and saying, "I will not have a parent advisory council in my school!" I said, "OK," and I was thinking to myself, "But one day you will."

At the end of the year, when we were having our last parent advisory council meeting, I was supposed to make the coffee or something and I forgot to do it, and that same principal said, "I can make the coffee, but don't tell my wife I did this."

He made the coffee, and he really enjoyed the meeting. In the end he came to appreciate the help the parents were able to provide.

When I was appointed parent coordinator by the Maryland State Department of Education, I asked someone from department, "What is a parent coordinator?" And I remember he said, "You'll find out."

Being a Title I Parent Coordinator was my first experience in "creating a job," an experience I went on to have several more times.

***

Every district had to have a parent advisory council that was made up of parents from the various schools. The president of our council was a parent named Chris who happened to be British. We used to travel to different meetings together because the state held parent meetings all over Maryland. Christ was a wonderful person, and she and I became good friends.

On one occasion we were going to attend a meeting in western Maryland. I was driving and she was riding with me, and I brought Todd along. On the way there, I said to Todd, "Did you pack my makeup bag?" Because I had asked him to put our bags in the car. He said, "No, I forgot it." There were almost no people of color living in western Maryland. As we drove along, we passed through this town and I said, "Well, I'm going to stop at the drugstore and see if I can find something."

At that time makeup for people of color was still scarce and at that store they had nothing in my color. Everything was peach or ivory. Chris said, "We are going to have to mix something up here." So, I bought a darker brown eyeshadow and a powder in peach or something and got a couple other things, and back at the hotel room later we mixed it together and that was my makeup.

Another memorable experience with Chris was when she and I and the assistant director of Title I, Mike, attended a Parent Conference in Detroit. We decided one day that we would go over to Canada because it was so close. Coming back from Canada, the guard at the border stopped us and asked for our credentials. Chris had forgotten hers, and they took us into a building and put Chris in an interrogation room. It was so scary.

Mike and I were outside the room waiting for her for hours as they questioned her. She called home and asked the babysitter to look in the drawer for her immigration papers to find her I.D. information. Finally, the border officers decided they would call the Immigration Service in Washington, DC. It was almost five o'clock and the federal offices all closed at five. Mike and I were sitting there, and I said, "I don't know if I have enough money to bail Chris out of jail."

Finally, to our great relief, one of the interrogators, who was more humane, let her go and we were able to leave. But that was something to experience! I will never forget it. They threatened to put her in jail. Mike and I were trying to figure out how we could scrounge up enough money to post bail. We were not going to leave her there.

To this day I'm not sure how she got out. I always say I can attest to the fact that the guards at the Canadian border are very astute.

***

As I look back on my teaching career, I can see how one opportunity led to another. During my time in Baltimore County with the Title I program, I was asked to be part of a committee with the Maryland State Department of Education, to create a TV reading series for four and five-year-olds. This was in the days of *Captain Kangaroo* and the beginning of educational children's programming. I served on the committee, and we created the television series, *Book, Look, and Listen.*

A director was hired, and a scriptwriter. Jerry, the director, needed a resource teacher, so he asked me if I would consider doing that. Excited by a new opportunity, of course, I said yes. I was released from the Baltimore County school system for one year to work on the series.

Jerry and I visited schools all over Maryland to determine what kinds of programs appealed to this age group. Information from the *Sesame Street* programs was also part of our research. We discovered that four and five-year-olds liked animal characters and enjoyed programs of fifteen to thirty minutes.

Based on our research, we created three characters: J. Worthington Book (who I named), representing books, Ethel Earphone, representing sound, and Hector Projector, representing film projectors. The series was developed in the early '70s, and to make it relevant to the times, Ethel was a female construction worker.

We hired professionals, and on Monday nights, we filmed at the public television studio until midnight. I was there for every filming. It was one of the most fascinating experiences for me. As we developed the series, I created the teacher's manual. I drafted some of the ideas for the illustrations, which were later done by a professional illustrator. The series evolved into thirty tele-lessons. So, instead of working on it for one year, I worked on the series for three years.

For one of the episodes, we wanted to show a giant panda bear. We called every toy store and finally found one at FAO Schwarz in New York. I was chosen to travel to pick it up. I was going to have to return by train with a giant panda sitting next to me. Fortunately, before I traveled to New York, we found one in Maryland.

Another time we wanted to use a llama in the program, so the zoo agreed to let us borrow a llama. Jerry and I drove to the zoo, and we picked up the llama in the television station's truck to bring llama back to the studio.

We stopped for gas on the way back, and the gas attendant almost dropped to the ground when he looked in the car. We hadn't realized the llama had walked up to the front of the van, so when the attendant looked in the window, he saw me, Jerry, and the llama! When we returned to the studio, it was my son's job to babysit the llama until the time for it to be filmed.

Simultaneously a TV series was being developed for third and fourth grade students. I had a chance to act in the series. That's when I decided that acting was hard work, and it was not something I wanted to do for a living!

Since we were using children's books, it was necessary to get copyright clearance from the author and the illustrator. In many cases they were two different people, and it was difficult sometimes to get permission from both. We had already filmed a sequence using a popular children's book since the author had given us permission to use it. But then we found out the illustrator said "No" to our request. That was so disappointing because we really wanted to use that book and share it with our viewing audience! We had to scrap the whole sequence and use another book.

In another situation we wanted to use the song "Happy Birthday." We found out it was still under copyright, and it took us six months to get permission to use the "Happy Birthday" song. When we put in our request to the copyright office in New York, we found out the copyright facilitator was out of the country traveling in Europe. So, we had to wait six months until she returned. She was the only one who could give us permission, and thankfully she did when she finally returned from her travels.

Another time we wanted to incorporate the "Grand Canyon Suite," as played by the New York Philharmonic Symphony. We found out in pursuing the copyright that we would have to pay each orchestra member their orchestra wages if we used their recording. Fortunately, there was a musician at the studio who was able to play it instead!

I learned so much about copyright laws and have been very conscious of it ever since. I don't think many people realize they are breaking copyright laws when they sing "Happy Birthday"!

The series was created through the auspices of the Division of Instructional Television in the Maryland State Department of Education. The division is no longer in existence, but I was looking back at the teacher's manual and found that some of the early literacy activities are just as relevant today as they were back then.

We were very conscious about making the series developmentally appropriate for the children who would be viewing it. Even after we began producing the series, we would take lessons to schools around the state and observe how the children responded to the program. We had a checklist when children watched, and we documented the amount of time that they watched.

Toward the end of the series, the contract for the writer expired, so I ended up writing the script for the last episode, and I really enjoyed it. Jerry and I shared an office and remained friends through the years. The whole thing was just a wonderful experience. I learned so much about production. We also won a Peabody Award for Excellence in Children's Programming!

ELEVEN

AFTER THE CLASSROOM

In 1983 after some changes in my personal life, I decided to take an early retirement from the Baltimore County School System and move to Washington, DC. I embarked on a new adventure both personally and career-wise. After being a classroom teacher and educator within the K-12 school system for more than twenty-five years, I entered the corporate sector for the first time, working with my brother, Ernest, and his business partner, Alexis Herman, in their consulting firm, Green-Herman & Associates.

Green-Herman & Associates

Ernest served the Carter Administration as Assistant Secretary of Labor and was responsible for creating the CETA (Comprehensive Employment and Training Act) Program. Alexis Herman also served the Carter administration as Director of the Labor Department's Women's Bureau. They formed their consulting company, Green-Herman & Associates, after President Reagan was elected and their service with the Carter administration ended.

The consulting firm was actively working with companies and large corporations to diversify their workforces and operate more equitably. When I first began working at Green-Herman, I asked my brother if I needed to go back to school for a business degree.

He replied, "You don't need an MBA, just use your common sense." That advice served me well and is a message I want to convey to young people: Trust yourself and try new things. Don't be afraid to go new places.

My first project at Green-Herman was with the Coca-Cola Company. When I was told that I would be in charge of the Coca-Cola project, I admit I was petrified. I knew what a Coke looked and tasted like, but my work experience was limited to public schools. I was charged with persuading Coca-Cola market development managers in several cities to sponsor summer day camps for underserved youth. In Richmond, Virginia, I said to the manager, "If young people have a fun, productive day in the hot summer, and they return home, wearing a Coca-Cola T-shirt, what do you suppose their parents will buy at the grocery store?" (Coca-Colas, of course.) Success! I applied my teaching skills, and it worked.

The Coca-Cola partnership provided many other exciting opportunities. Once I was asked to represent Coca-Cola at a program in Washington, DC for market development managers who serviced Korean-owned stores. I was seated on the stage with other participants, and the entire program was in Korean. Being totally unfamiliar with the language, I asked how was I to know when it was time for my presentation? I was told to listen for my name; I did, and the program proceeded smoothly. I was also invited, several times, to attend the Market Development Managers Seminar, at the Atlanta headquarters. I was always impressed with the amount of research required to develop marketing strategies. They were very much like strategies a teacher must develop to maintain interest in the classroom!

***

Another experience during that time was the passing of Daisy Bates' husband, L.C. Bates. My brother Ernest, and Reverend Jesse Jackson were to attend his funeral and speak. Neither of them could attend, unfortunately, so both told me that I would represent them. I wrote and delivered the remarks for each of them, and after the service, this lady came up to me and said, "That sounded just like Reverend Jackson." That let me know I had done my job!

The last time I saw Daisy Bates, was in Washington at the Smithsonian. The Smithsonian Museum opened an exhibit on Women and Civil Rights. She was one of the women cited in the exhibit and was present at the opening reception. Civil rights pioneer, Dr. Dorothy Height, was also in the exhibit. Ernest and I attended the reception, then went to the hotel where Mrs. Bates was staying, and spent some time with her. She was in a wheelchair at that time and not long after that she passed. Her funeral occurred on the same day the Little Rock Nine were presented with the Congressional Gold Medal by President Clinton at the White House.

***

In 1984 Reverend Jesse Jackson earned enough support in the primaries to become a viable presidential candidate, and he chose Green-Herman to facilitate his quest for the presidency. Prior to the Democratic National Convention, I remember keeping record of Candidate Jackson's many, many speaking engagements. At the convention in San Francisco, I was assigned to assist Mrs. Jackson. I spent much time in the Jacksons' hotel suite – answering the phone, and the door, and accompanying her to events. We spent one entire day at a local TV studio, preparing the video to be shown prior to Reverend Jackson's primary speech. The night of the speech, Mrs. Jackson chose not to attend, but to watch in the candidate's trailer. She invited me to watch with her, and another guest – actress Cicely Tyson! What a memorable week.

National Council of Negro Women

After working with the Green-Herman firm for a couple of years, Alexis and Ernest were approached by civil rights pioneer, Dr. Dorothy Height, and she asked them if I could work with her on a special project. Dr. Height was president of the National Council of Negro Women. NCNW had received a grant from the U.S. Department of Transportation to create a "Minority Women in Transportation Program." Little had been accomplished, so Dr. Height asked me to help rescue the program. We had less than year before funding expired.

Fortunately, I was able to connect with the National Minority Transit Association, which enabled me to facilitate transit seminars for minority college women in Ohio, Washington, DC, and Atlanta. In addition, we published the first research document, "Minority Women in Transit."

It was a great privilege to work for Dr. Height at the National Council of Negro Women. She had advised many leaders, including Eleanor Roosevelt, President Eisenhower, and President Johnson. She played a leading role in organizing Dr. Martin Luther King Jr.'s March on Washington in 1963. She was the most elegant person and had a persona of royalty. In fact, one of her friends who worked with her for years would say, "She could always find a 'throne,' the subjects would come to her, and she would hold court."

During the time that I worked with Dr. Height at the NCNW, the Martin Luther King, Jr. holiday was being finalized by Congress. Dr. Height asked me to represent NCNW at one of the final planning meetings. Mrs. Coretta Scott King was also present at this meeting. A big celebration to "kick off" the King Holiday was scheduled at the Kennedy Center, and I attended the celebration with Dr. Height. The event featured several entertainers, including Stevie Wonder, who serenaded the gathering with his famous rendition of "Happy Birthday."

Once, my brother and I were at a conference and Dr. Height entered. I whispered to Ernest, "How long do you think it's going to take her to get a seat on the stage?" Soon after she entered, someone realized she was there, and she was immediately escorted to the stage. She had a very large presence and was highly respected. It was quite an honor to work with her.

While working with NCNW, Dr. Height asked me to represent the organization at meetings of the American Association for the Advancement of Science (AAAS), since I had public school teaching experience. I was happy to do so. In fact, that experience positioned me for my next career.

American Association for the Advancement of Science

As the NCNW Transit Program was ending, I was offered a position with AAAS. My responsibility was to work with community groups, nationally, to develop programs that would "hook" students and others to "like" science. This was a perfect challenge for me, as science was my least favorite subject in school!

A highlight of this experience was the creation of the "Black Church Program." This program, conducted in churches throughout the country, trained members who provided tutoring support in reading to also provide support for science courses. At this time, I also worked with the Chicago Museum of Science and

Industry to launch the "Black Science Achievers" exhibit. I helped to coordinate activities involving the community, which were conducted in Chicago, and later, in Los Angeles, when the exhibit moved there. Working with community-based organizations, like the National Urban League, created additional opportunities to participate in and speak at their national conferences.

Association of Science/Technology Centers

Work at AAAS led to collaboration with the Association of Science-Technology Centers (ASTC). ASTC received a grant from the Carnegie Foundation to assist science centers to diversify their staffs, boards, and visitors. This became the "Community Group Partnership Program," and I was appointed co-director. I traveled to science centers and museums across the country, conducting workshops to address those issues. As a result of this experience, I developed a close working relationship with the Texas Museum Association. As one of the largest museum associations in the country, the annual conference was attended by several hundred museum workers. I was honored to be invited several times as a presenter.

***

In 1991 my former husband passed suddenly, and my son Todd was at the house with him when it happened. He called me immediately, and I knew it was very upsetting to him. I ended up being the one to organize all the funeral arrangements.

I was working with the ASTC at that time and was to be the keynote speaker at the Texas Museums Association Conference, in Corpus Christi, Texas. I flew from Baltimore, the morning after the funeral, to Corpus Christi for the conference. One of the first events that night was the opening reception at an art museum.

Shortly after I arrived, and greeted many friends, I began to have problems walking. I literally could not walk. I was then helped to the shuttle bus, to return to the hotel.

My responsibility at the conference was to attend all the workshops, do an analysis, and then on the last day provide guidance as to how they could continue to diversify museum programs, visitors, staffs and boards. Due to my immobile status, the conference organizers taped all of the sessions for me, and I made notes in my hotel room.

The morning of the day I was to make the speech, I was taken to the hospital emergency room in Corpus Christi. The doctor, after a brief examination, asked, "Do you know how to walk on crutches?" I replied, "No." He responded, "Well, you're going to learn how." I began to realize that my immobility was probably a psychological reaction to the trauma of the last several days. I was taken back to the hotel for my speech, to be delivered immediately following lunch. My entrance to the ballroom stage was in a wheelchair! My speech went well and following the event, a friend said, "Treopia, I've heard of dramatic entrances, but yours beats everything!" After returning home and resting more, full use of my legs returned, thankfully.

***

Following the Texas conference, I continued my work with ASTC, commuting every day from Baltimore to Washington. During this period, my son and I began a multitude of renovation projects. Fortunately, he was able to help a lot with the work, and I was able to pursue my hobby of interior decorating. However, driving back and forth between the house in Baltimore and my job in Washington DC was draining, but it was important to provide the necessary support for my son, during this period. Shortly after, I was in the hair salon talking to another customer. She informed me that she was the Director of Education for the National Office of the NAACP located in Baltimore. She explained that she needed an education coordinator and asked if I would take the position. I was able to leave ASTC and take that position at the NAACP, which was only twenty-five minutes from my house. This work experience was the closest I ever had to my home.

NAACP National Office

One of the highlights during my work as an education program coordinator with the NAACP was when I represented the organization at Mae Jemison's space launch in the shuttle *Endeavor*. This was historic because Mae Jemison was the first Black woman to travel in space. Todd and I flew to Florida and stayed in Orlando to see the launch at Cape Canaveral. The night prior to the launch, a dinner was held to honor the astronauts. Of course, they were not present, since they were preparing for the next-day launch. I had the honor of sitting at the table with Ms. Jemison's 5th grade teacher from Chicago, her hometown. Very early the following morning, the shuttle bus picked us up at the hotel, and drove us to the launch site. We arrived early enough to explore the area a bit. We were then seated on bleachers across the inlet from the launch site. I will never forget the earth shaking and the roaring sound, as the rocket, *Endeavor*, soared into space. What a thrill!

Columbus Center for Marine Research and Exploration

During my time working for the NAACP, I met the Director of the Columbus Center, a new science center and museum, being developed in Baltimore's Inner Harbor. The center was created to collaborate with the University of Maryland Center of Marine Biotechnology. He offered me the position of education director. Again, the timing worked. The NAACP was under new leadership, and changes were in order. I accepted the offer—another new challenge and opportunity at the new museum. However, not being a science person, I really had to memorize saying the phrase, "a collaboration with the Center of Marine Biotechnology!"

My responsibility was, again, to help defuse the stereotype of science to the public. I created opportunities for classes to meet with the University of Maryland scientists. I would ask the scientists to wear jeans, not their white lab coats. I wanted the students to see the scientists as "real" people, and not the stereotype of a goofy person wearing a white coat and high-water pants.

One time I was asked to be a judge at the first science fair ever held at this particular middle school. A student, a little girl, had an exhibit about "bioremediation." I asked her, "What inspired you to do this?" She said, "I learned about it at the Columbus Center." She had been in one of the classes I worked with. Triumph! Her teacher, who brought his class regularly, retired, and then worked as a greeter at Home Depot. When I shopped there, he would introduce me to his colleagues as, "the person who helped my students to like science."

Another success was an invitation to speak to parents at a low-income housing project. This evolved from many conversations with members of that community. I realized that many of the children (and parents) had not been to the Inner Harbor, although they lived literally right across the street. As a result, I created several Saturday experiences for families who lived in the housing project.

Unfortunately, the Columbus Center closed suddenly on December 24, 1996, due to unsolvable financial issues. It was a great disappointment for me personally since I enjoyed my work there very much and felt we were making a difference for students, who had not previously made personal connections to the field of science. When the center closed, I and the rest of the staff lost our jobs and became unemployed right before the holidays. For the first time in my adult life, I did not have a job.

Following the New Year, I began to contemplate, "'What is next?" I decided to call to someone I knew, who was President Clinton's Director of Personnel, and who had visited Columbus Center. When I explained what had happened, I was invited to meet at his office. Following the meeting, I was offered a Presidential appointment with the White House Initiative on Historically Black Colleges and Universities (HBCUs). I was thrilled, and eagerly accepted. HBCUs have been very important to our family.

White House Initiative on Historically Black Colleges and Universities

I enjoyed many wonderful experiences during this appointment. My responsibilities included: helping to plan activities for National HBCU Week and planning the President's Advisory Board Meeting. This experience provided the opportunity to meet and work with many presidents of HBCUs.

As the Clinton Administration ended, I, like all other presidential appointees, knew we would need to find new jobs. About that time, I received a message from someone I had recently met, asking if I knew anything about the National Board for Professional Teaching Standards (NBPTS). I replied that I did not. She told me that they were looking for someone who fit my qualifications and suggested that I contact them. I did, and an interview with the director was scheduled. To my surprise, the director knew my brother, Ernest. When he was in the U.S. Labor Department and she was in the Florida State Education Department, he assisted with funding for her department. Our meeting concluded with an offer to become Vice President of Partnerships and Minority Affairs at NBPTS. This was an offer I could not refuse!

National Board for Professional Teaching Standards

When I started working at the National Board for Professional Teaching Standards, I was assigned to work with South Dakota and Arkansas. I knew I wanted to learn more about the Indigenous Americans of South Dakota, the Oceti Sakowin. An opportunity came when I heard about a meeting to be conducted by a colleague in the U.S. Department of Education and held at the Pine Ridge Reservation in South Dakota.

My long-lasting, permanent relationship with South Dakota started with this meeting. It helped me to learn more about the struggles the Lakota faced. I just wish other people, especially lawmakers, would seek out that opportunity as well. As I listened and learned during the meeting all I could think of was, "This was their country; they were here first. How horrible to be relegated to this kind of existence."

At the meeting, I met the NBPTS Coordinator in South Dakota, who invited me to speak at the upcoming summer meeting of the state's National Board Certified Teachers (NBCTs). I couldn't wait to return to South Dakota! The meeting was held in Chamberlain, South Dakota, and following the meeting, I was invited to join a group for dinner at a restaurant on the Missouri River. The setting was so beautiful. The group included education administrators, the Secretary of Education Dr. Melody Schopp (who became my dear friend), and one of the speakers, a professor from the University of Wyoming.

As we talked, I mentioned that my home was Little Rock, Arkansas. The professor said that he was also from Arkansas. As we talked further, I said that my brother was one of the nine students who integrated Little Rock Central High School. The professor, who was White, then said, "Your brother changed my life." A hush fell over the entire group, all were in shock.

The professor went on to say that when Ernest was going through that year, he followed him intensely in the news. He began to realize that he was more like Ernest than he had imagined. He added that his father and grandfather thought differently. For me, that needed no further explanation, and I surmised they had been against integration. I saw the professor years later, and he said, "You won't believe this, but my father voted for President Obama." Miracles never cease!

***

During the course of my trips to South Dakota, my son Todd would sometimes accompany me, and we made many friends in the education community. Our friend, Dr. Joe Hauge, would plan wonderful sight-seeing ventures for us. On one of those trips, Joe asked if we would like to see buffalo. Of course, Todd and I were very excited, because that is not something we could experience in Baltimore!

Joe drove us to Custer State Park, where we immediately spotted a buffalo herd on the hillside. We slowed down long enough for me to snap pictures. After touring the beautiful park, we were on a single-lane road to leave. Suddenly, the small car was surrounded by four huge buffalo, one on each side of the car. The one on the passenger side pressed its face close enough to the window that I could see the eyes. I quietly asked Joe, "What do we do now?" He replied, "We sit still and wait until they leave." (I think my son had stopped breathing.) Shortly after, the buffalo left, and we continued our journey. Since that time, I don't mention the word "buffalo" to Todd!

For many people on the East Coast, South Dakota might as well be Europe. It is that foreign to them. I've actually been to South Dakota more than any other place in all my travels for work. It is one of my favorite places to visit, and I have come to love it especially because of the friends I've made there. I don't miss the blizzards though—on my last trip we were snowed in for three days and that was in April!

Somebody in Baltimore said to me, "We've had snow before!" I replied, "You don't know what a blizzard is until you've experienced one in South Dakota! You literally can't see anything, and you can't do anything, and you can't go anywhere!" We were snowbound at the Holiday Inn in Rapid City and got to know everybody in the hotel on a first-name basis.

***

I had many enjoyable travel experiences during my time with the National Board, including trips to Hawaii and Alaska. On one particularly memorable trip for NBPTS, I traveled to Phoenix to attend the NALEO Conference. This was the year prior to the presidential election in 2000, and the Democratic presidential candidates were at the National Association of Elected and Appointed Latino Officials (NALEO) Conference. I had joined NALEO as part of my outreach for my position at National Board. My colleague and I went to the session to hear the candidates. Each time one was introduced they would try to say something in

Spanish. My colleague, who was Latina, said, "They should just stop trying because they're saying it all wrong!"

When Reverend Al Sharpton, who was one of the candidates, got up to speak he said, "I'm not going to try to say anything in Spanish, but I'm going to talk about people who are doing things to people who speak Spanish." He received a long standing ovation. I've never met Reverend Sharpton, but from that time, I have wanted to let him know that that was when I first became a fan of his.

The other thing I remember about that trip was that it was 117 degrees in Phoenix. The heat was unbearable! I remember telling somebody that, and they said, "But it's a dry heat." I said, "Well, dry heat is hot heat!"

***

I was working for the National Board when 9/11 occurred, and our office building was in Arlington, Virginia. I was driving to work and had the radio on when they announced the first plane, American Airlines Flight 11, had hit the North Tower of the World Trade Center. It was unclear what was happening, whether it was an accident or intentional.

When I got to the office, everybody was standing around the television, and a young staff member said there was an accident. Then while we were watching the television, we saw the second plane, United Airlines Flight 175, hit the South Tower, and we knew, no, that was no accident. Then they announced a third plane had hit the Pentagon. We looked out the window and could see the smoke coming from that direction.

Our director was at our office in Michigan that day, and so the assistant director turned to me and said, "What do you think we ought to do?" Then the announcement came over the intercom that the building had to be evacuated immediately. There must have been about ninety offices in our building, and everybody went to the parking garage at the same time, so it took me forty minutes to get out of the garage.

I had four people from our staff with me in my car because we all lived in Maryland, and they had taken public transportation and needed rides. We stopped to get gas and then started driving, but all the bridges were closed around Washington, so I had to drive all the way up to Northern Virginia to get on the highway to come back to Maryland. There were thousands of people on the road evacuating, and a trip that usually took one hour took me four hours. I felt so apprehensive on the drive because America was under attack, and we didn't know what would happen next.

When I arrived in my driveway finally, my hands were clenching the steering wheel and my legs wouldn't move. It was as though I was frozen. My son had to come and help me out of the car and into the house. Todd kept saying, "Take it easy, it's ok." I was in shock. I guess that is the most frightened I have ever been in my life.

While driving home, I had remembered Ernest was in New York and had a meeting scheduled at the World Trade Center that morning. I hadn't heard from him, so I didn't know if he had gone up the night before or flown up that morning. I called his secretary and she said he had gone up the night before and stayed in a hotel and then was going to his meeting at the World Trade Center.

I was finally able to connect with Ernest by phone later that day and found out that he had arisen early and decided to stop at a restaurant to have breakfast. While he was eating breakfast, the first plane hit. If he had not decided to make that stop, he would have been in the building when the plane hit. He was one of the lucky ones, but it was a horrific day, and I will never, ever forget it.

Bowie State University, College of Education

On the afternoon of Friday, June 17, 2011, I was at home, having taken the day off. The phone rang, and when I answered, the person on the other end announced that she was the Director of Human Resources at NBPTS. She went on to say, "NBPTS has decided to eliminate ten positions, and yours is one of them." After temporarily recovering from shock, I asked, "When is my last day?" She answered, "Today."

I immediately remembered the meeting scheduled for Monday, with the Dean of the College of Education at Bowie State University, an HBCU in Maryland. Dean Taylor and I had talked several times, and she had expressed great interest in incorporating NBPTS Standards in the College of Education curriculum. I tried to call Dean Taylor, but it was late, and her office was closed for the day. It became apparent that I would keep our scheduled meeting.

When I arrived for the meeting on Monday morning, I said to the dean, "I need to share what just happened, as it will impact our plans." As I described Friday's experience, she began to smile. She responded, "I am just waiting for you to finish because I have lots of things I would like you to help me with." Thus began my work with Bowie and the initiation of a brand-new position: Director of Special Initiatives, and the start of my fourteenth career.

Although I began work on a consulting basis, the position soon morphed into a full-time role. This has been a wonderful, different experience. The opportunity to work with faculty, staff and students has been rewarding. I have had the opportunity to coordinate many events, including American Education Week, Black History Month, Women's History Month, and Service Awards programs. I have also served on college-wide committees. Although leadership roles have changed, I have enjoyed extraordinary support from all in those positions, especially from our current Dean, Dr. Rhonda Jeter.

Although my HBCU alma mater is Hampton University, Bowie will always have a special place in my heart.

***

One of the ways we were brought up was to always act your best and do your best wherever you are and whatever you are doing because you never know where it might lead you. I have tried to maintain my relationships and keep up connections with people over the years. In my work with national organizations, I have been able to visit almost every state in our country. I would always try to see what Hampton alumni lived in the city I was going to, and I'd usually try to connect with them. Even if we hadn't known each other while in school, we had the shared bond of being Hampton alumni.

In reflecting about the jobs and positions which I've been fortunate enough to have, I realized I have only applied for two or three jobs and was offered all the other positions. For most of the fourteen careers I've had, one job has led seamlessly to another. I trace that success back to my childhood, learning how to interact positively and diplomatically with people, doing your best no matter what situation you're in, and being confident enough in yourself to take on new challenges. We were encouraged to try new things—that's how you learn.

Through the years and careers, my son, Todd, has been my right and left hand. He just knows what to do and does things before even being asked. I have been able to continue working professionally because of the help he provides me. He is extremely thoughtful and knows how to take care of everything—the car, the house, even some meals. Every morning he brings me a cup of coffee and the morning paper. We take two newspapers daily, the *Washington Post* and the *Baltimore Sun*. We both follow politics and current events and enjoy discussing the news of the day. Often, he'll find an article for me to be sure to read. We are both Baltimore Ravens fans and love to watch football games. I couldn't ask for a better person as a son.

TWELVE

SPECIAL EXPERIENCES

Throughout my life, I've had the opportunity meet some remarkable individuals and work on inspiring projects. These are some of those special experiences:

Working with Oprah

When I was working as Title I Parent Coordinator for Baltimore County Public Schools, I learned of the National Coalition of Title I Parents. It was an organization of parents who were having difficulty penetrating the schools' organizational structures, as federal law intended. I found the organization very helpful and learned a lot from them.

At the National Coalition's annual conference in Cleveland, Ohio, I happened to see Oprah Winfrey in the hotel lobby. I recognized Oprah because she had just started as a news anchor on a TV station in Baltimore. I introduced myself, and said, "What are you doing here? I live in Baltimore." And she said that Reverend Jesse Jackson had asked her to organize a PUSH Excel Rally in Baltimore, and then she asked if I would help her. I said, "Sure," but I really didn't expect to hear from her again.

Several weeks later, I was in my office, and the phone rang. The secretary said, "Oprah Winfrey is on the phone for you." So, that's how it started.

We worked together for about a year and pulled off the rally at the Civic Center downtown. It was very successful and was coordinated with the Baltimore City Schools. During that year we met frequently and talked on the phone. I also had Oprah as a speaker at a couple of my big Title I Parents' Advisory Council meetings, and she was outstanding. She was so vivacious and enthusiastic, and everyone just loved it. I knew it would not be long before she moved on. And it happened—that was just before she went to Chicago.

I remember one Saturday Oprah came to my house to wrap up something related to the PUSH Excel Rally. She left her purse when she rushed out. My son said, "Mom, Oprah Winfrey left her purse." I said, "Don't worry, stand at the door with her purse, she'll be back." Sure enough, a couple of minutes later, we heard this screech of auto brakes in front of the house—it was Oprah!

In fact, my neighbor still talks about that—the day that Oprah Winfrey came to my house.

It was a terrific year. At the end of the year after the PUSH Excel Rally was over, Oprah had a dinner at her house in the Village of Cross Keys. Her mother was there and one of the other TV anchors, his wife, and me. Soon after, she left for Chicago to start *The Oprah Winfrey Show*.

I saw Oprah twice after that. My brother and Alexis Herman had a consulting firm at the time and were conducting the Black Mayors Conference in Atlantic City, and Oprah Winfrey was one of the speakers. I had just begun working with the consulting firm. When she arrived, she asked, "Where's Tre girl?"

Then I saw her a couple of years later at a reception in Washington, DC. I took a picture with her then and I still have it in my family room.

We spent a lot of time together that year and had a really good connection. I also had her as a speaker at my church. A couple of years ago, one of the older ladies in my church said, "Do you think you can get Oprah Winfrey back as a guest?" I said, "I think that ship has sailed."

The Ernest Green Story

The Disney studios decided to create a film detailing Ernest's experiences at Little Rock Central High School, as one of the Little Rock Nine, and the only senior. When the screenwriter, was developing the script, he always sent it to Ernest to review for authenticity before it was finalized. I met with the screenwriter several times. I remember he once asked me, "What were some of the songs that were popular at the time?" We spent quite a bit of time with him; he wanted to make sure to get the story right and true to the facts.

Some poetic license was taken in the film. For example, the characterization of our grandfather, played by Ossie Davis, was more a combination of my aunt and grandfather's personalities Another example, our neighbor, portrayed by the actress Ruby Dee, was actually a male neighbor. When Ernest first started at Central, this neighbor confronted Ernest one day and said in essence, "What is the matter with you? You are messing things up for us. We have good jobs, and many of us own our own homes, and here you are over there just messing things up." This neighbor had never said much before, but he was really upset with Ernest and reflected a "don't rock the boat" attitude that some people had.

The film premiered on the Disney Channel, January 17, 1993. Prior to that premier, Disney hosted two gala premieres in Little Rock, on January 9. Governor Bill Clinton just elected 42nd U.S. President, and close friend of Ernest, insisted that the receptions be held before he left for Washington. Disney constructed a movie theater in the auditorium at Little Rock Central High School with materials from five flat-trucks, driven across country from California. The first reception was held in the afternoon for students. The second reception, that evening, was an "invitation only" event for the public and Disney personnel, attended by President Clinton and Ernest.

I was working with the NAACP National Convention when the film was released. I was able to have Ernest and Morris Chesnut, the actor who played him in the film, present for the NAACP Youth portion of the convention. *The Ernest Green Story* was shown, and immediately after it ended, the stage curtain was raised, and Ernest and Morris were standing there. The crowd of students went wild! They were so excited to see them standing there in real life, after just viewing the film.

Disney Teachers Awards

During my time at the National Board of Professional Teaching Standards, one of the staff people who had preceded me was a judge for the Disney Teacher Awards. Each year Disney awarded several teachers at a gala awards event that was televised. My colleague asked if I would like to take over as judge, since I was formerly a teacher. I was happy to do so. As a result, I served for four years as a national judge for the Disney Teacher Awards program.

Each spring we were flown to Disney World in Florida, to spend three days for the preliminary selection. Our task was to select the forty finalists from the final two hundred entries. Originally, there were thousands of entries. The awards event was held in the summer, in Disneyland, California. The Disney Corporation would fly all the judges, teacher finalists, and our families to Disneyland for a week. When our plane arrived at Los Angeles International Airport the attendant would announce, "The Disney Corporation is here to pick up the Disney guests." We would get off the plane first and then be met by uniformed chauffeurs, led to a limousine, and driven to Disneyland from the airport.

We always stayed at the Grand Californian Hotel, the largest hotel in Disneyland. The hospitality was indescribable. Each night, Disney would have a surprise for us in our room—a little gift and something edible, usually in the shape of Mickey Mouse ears. However, each time my son and I stayed at the hotel, on the first day of our arrival, I would make a point of walking around the entire hotel property with Todd to make sure that hotel staff understood that Todd was with me and a guest of the hotel. I wanted him to be able to go swimming and do things by himself without being bothered or questioned, "Why are you here?" I knew if I did not do that the assumption might be that he was there unlawfully. This is a protective measure many Black mothers learn to take for their children.

During the day at the beginning of the week, the other judges and I were busy selecting the award winners. It was a job! But we still had time to enjoy Disneyland. We were each assigned a Disney Guide for all the Disney rides and attractions. The guide would take us to whatever rides we wanted to go to, and, of course, we were always in the front of the line. Each evening, Disney planned an extraordinary experience for the entire group, and each evening ended with a fabulous gift. They rolled out the red carpet every day. I don't know if I could ever go to Disneyland again as a regular tourist!

The evening before the final day, Disney hosted a formal dinner. At this dinner, the winning teacher was announced. The official dinner hosts were the Disney characters: Mickey and Minnie Mouse, Donald Duck, and others. On the final day, the teachers, in a specially decorated bus, were honorees in the Disney Parade, with thousands of people standing there waving. The parade ended with the teachers seated in front of the Castle for a special program. For the teachers, it was a marvelous experience to be honored like that. I still stay in touch with some of the teachers who were contestants at that time.

Monash University

At a research conference I attended for Bowie State, I met the Dean of Education at Monash University, one of the top fifty universities in the world and located in Melbourne, Australia. The dean and I began to talk, and during our conversation I found out that his son was attending medical school at the University of Arkansas, in Little Rock. Of course, I told him about my family and everything we experienced in Little Rock. Shortly after that I heard from him again. He said Monash University was celebrating their 50th anniversary, and he invited me to be the keynote speaker. I accepted and several months later was on a fifteen-hour flight on Qantas Airlines from California to Melbourne!

The flight was very comfortable, but I tried not to think about how many hours we were over the ocean. I always pack two watches when I travel, so that I can set my watch to the correct time zone when I arrive at my destination. When I arrived in Australia, I did my usual and took out my second watch, as there is a seventeen-hour time difference from Eastern Standard Time. One day when I was there, I had a little extra time and decided to shop for some souvenirs. I was on a main street and as I walked, I kept bumping into people.

I said to myself, "I am doing something wrong."

So, I decided to lean back against a building and observe. I realized that people there did everything from the left, whereas in America we do things from the right. After I got the hang of it, I re-entered the pedestrian traffic, but when I got to the street corner, I decided I better wait until a crowd crossed and go with them. I didn't want to risk walking the wrong way in the street!

I had an extraordinary experience at Monash University. On one of the days the Dean had a luncheon with some of the College of Education staff, and one of the staff members told me, "We could tell that Dean had talked with you because when he came back to campus, he had a totally new perspective on the Aboriginal community." The school has a large Indigenous Studies program, and I was very interested to learn more about that while I was there.

While visiting Melbourne, I also had the opportunity to reconnect with someone I met when attending an art exhibit at the Australian Embassy in Washington, DC. A former colleague of mine was working at the embassy, and he invited me. During the exhibit an Australian author, who had written a book about Little Rock, spoke. After he finished, I approached the lectern and said, "You were talking about my family. My brother was one of the students that you have written about in your book." He was blown away. In fact, he said, "You are royalty!" We kept in touch, and while I was in Melbourne, he and his wife invited me to their home for dinner.

I will never forget the wonderful people in Melbourne, and the memorable time I spent "Down Under."

Congressman John Lewis Experience

The year before he passed, I had the opportunity to visit Congressman John Lewis's office. Congressman Lewis was linked with my family in many ways. Those links are directly related to my brother, Ernest, and his experiences as one of the Little Rock Nine. Ernest first met John Lewis during the '60s civil rights struggle. Congressman Lewis, whose experiences are well documented, told Ernest that he was inspired by the endurance and fortitude demonstrated by Ernest during the 1957 integration crisis at Central High School. In 2007, during the 50th Anniversary Celebration of the 1957 Integration Crisis, the National Park Service dedicated the new Little Rock Central High School Historic Site. The keynote speaker for the dedication of this new museum was Congressman John Lewis.

Fast forward to the spring of 2019. I received a call from a Hartford, Connecticut teacher, whom I remembered talking with at the 60th Anniversary Celebration of the '57 Crisis, in 2017. He explained that five of his middle school students were entering the National History Contest. Their topic was the Little Rock Central High School 1957 Integration Crisis, and they wanted to interview me. Of course, I was delighted to help.

After several telephone discussions, their original dramatization, *Paying a Price for Education*, was completed. The entry won first place in the Hartford city contest. Next, it won second place in the Connecticut state contest, which qualified them to enter the National History Contest. That competition was held at the University of Maryland. The really exciting news, however, was the invitation from Congressman John Lewis, to perform their entry for him at his office! I was invited, with my son, to attend the event as special guests.

On the day of the presentation, Congressman Lewis arrived at his office, after casting a vote in the House. He then invited us into his conference room. Truly memorable, was his command to his entire staff, to stop whatever they were doing and come to the presentation. Several staffers mentioned work that needed to be done, but the Congressman insisted that this was more important, something they needed to learn about.

The students did a wonderful job; in fact, they almost brought me to tears. After the production, we were invited to take several pictures with Congressman Lewis. I will treasure mine forever. The Congressman then inquired about my brother, Ernest, and asked that I let him know he asked about him.

John Lewis was truly a "Gentle Giant." I will always remember him as one whose humility and grace are as memorable as his outstanding contributions to the pursuit of equity and equality for the citizens of this country.

Mandela Moments

Although I did not meet South African President Nelson Mandela personally, I did have two very special "Mandela moments."

In 1990, I was working with the American Association for the Advancement of Science (AAAS), headquartered in Washington, DC, and was conducting a science project with the Jefferson Parish Public Schools in New Orleans. On this day, February 2, I was preparing to leave the Hilton Hotel to return to Washington, having spent three or four days, attending project-related events. My bags were packed, and I was waiting for the bellman, ready to head to the airport. The TV was on, and while I waited, suddenly there was a newsflash. The announcer exclaimed, "Nelson Mandela is free, and is leaving the prison where he has spent the last twenty-seven years." At that moment, the bellman knocked on the door, I let him in, and both of us stood there, not believing what we were hearing and seeing. I was almost late for my plane, but had to stay and listen to the details—what a moment!

During my experience as a Clinton presidential appointee with the White House Initiative on HBCUs, I was part of a group, including the director and several HBCU presidents, who were invited to the White House during National HBCU Week. The event was held to honor President Nelson Mandela and his wife, who were visiting President Clinton. We were sitting in the Gold Room, along with hordes of press reporters and photographers, when President Clinton escorted the Mandelas to the stage. I remember President Mandela as being so very elegant, yet warm and humble. As he took the mic, everyone was in awe. I will never forget his words "President Clinton, the people of South Africa love you." The room broke into applause, for at that moment, those words meant so much.

Meeting Presidents

In addition to meeting President Truman as a child, I have had the opportunity to meet several other presidents. When Ernest served as Assistant Secretary of Labor in President Carter's administration, I went to the White House on the day that Andrew Young was sworn in as the United States Ambassador to the United Nations. Young was a leader in the civil rights movement and the first Black person to hold the ambassadorship to the United Nations. Ernest was attending the ceremony and asked if I'd like to join him as his guest, and that's when I met President Carter.

***

I met President Clinton first when he was governor in the '70s in Little Rock. My brother Ernest knew him and was friends with him. One time when he was governor, I saw him at a reception in Washington. I was behind him in line and touched him on the shoulder and said, "Hello, Governor, how are you?" He turned around and greeted me by name and went on to name the school and the city, where we had been on a panel together. The event had taken place several years before in Marianna, Arkansas! I was blown away that he would remember my name and so many details.

Several of my friends were involved in working on Clinton's campaign for president. I was an enthusiastic supporter of his campaign. I always made a point of wearing a large button that said "I'm from Arkansas! Ask me about my Governor!" whenever I would go out shopping. It was a great conversation starter. People would stop and ask me, and I would have a chance to talk with them about all the reasons why I felt Clinton would make a great president. I think those buttons were a very effective campaign tool!

On the day of the election after Todd and I voted near our home in Baltimore, I started thinking. I was so excited about him running and I told Todd, "You know I think I want to go down to Little Rock. I want to be there." I called and got us tickets—that was in the olden days before there was so much security at airports. We were able to get a plane to Little Rock and on the flight there were people who had been involved in the campaign also going down for election night.

We arrived in the late afternoon around 5:00. Then we went and picked up our family friend, my surrogate mother, Lucille, and went directly in front of the State House where the election results were going to be shown. Eventually the Clinton family came out front and Governor and Mrs. Clinton and their daughter, Chelsea, were standing there, and the minute his numbers went over the top, the crowd went wild. It was the most exciting thing to be there when the election was called, and he won.

We attended Clinton's first inauguration with Ernest. The church service which always precedes the swearing in was held at my brother's church in Washington. We had to get there to stand in line at six in the morning. Our Little Rock friend, and famous jazz musician, Art Porter Sr., played at the service. After that we were invited to observe the presidential parade from the Marriott Hotel, and we stood on the balcony to watch.

That night I attended the presidential ball and wore a formal ball gown. It was another "once in a lifetime" type of experience, and I felt privileged to be a part of it.

***

Several years ago, I had the opportunity to meet President George W. Bush. There was a program called the "Presidential Scholars Program" for members of the corporate world. It was a joint program between the Clinton and Bush Presidential Libraries. There was a graduation of the scholars in Little Rock at Central High School, and Ernest made sure that my son and I were invited.

We went straight from the airport to Central where the graduation was held. After the ceremony there was a dinner at the Clinton Library, and that's where I met President George W. Bush and his wife, Laura. I was sitting at a table not too far from the door, and when they were getting ready to leave, I just got up and went over and met them at the door. I introduced myself, and said I was Ernest Green's sister. He stopped and spoke with me for a moment, and I was very pleased to have met him.

The Green Siblings Project

A highlight of my time with the National Board of Professional Teaching Standards was meeting Sharla Steever, who was a National Board Certified Teacher in South Dakota. Later I met Sharla's colleague Dr. Scott Simpson, and I was invited to speak at the region's largest educational conference. Ernest was invited to South Dakota as an education conference keynote speaker also.

My professional relationship with Sharla and Scott blossomed into a friendship and a creative collaboration dear to my heart. Sharla, Scott, and I began to discuss the development of a project about my family. Thus evolved, the "Green Siblings Project." It consists of a website sharing a series of interviews with my brothers and me along with other supportive educational materials.

Scott and Sharla also created a Green Siblings documentary screened at several film festivals and events. During the summer of 2019, Sharla and Scott flew to my home in Baltimore, to interview my brother Scott, who came down from New York by train for the day. That was the last time I saw him before he passed on April 12, 2020. It means so much to have those last images of my brother.

January 4, 2011

Dear Chancellor Gearhart:

I am a native Arkansan and have long awaited an opportunity to share this concern, and perhaps make a request. This message is also on behalf of my two brothers: Ernest Green, one of the Little Rock Nine, the only senior and first Black graduate of Little Rock Central High School; and my brother Scott Green – first Black member of the New York City Sheet Metal Workers Union #28. In 1951, our mother Lothaire Scott Green, was awarded a Master of Education degree from UA, but was denied the opportunity to participate in graduation ceremonies. I remember vividly the day the postman delivered the box with her diploma, hood, and a letter acknowledging her accomplishment, yet informing her that she would be unwelcome on campus. I shall never forget the look of hurt and disgust in her eyes as she silently crumpled the letter and threw it in the trash. As the years passed, particularly after her death in 1976, we have wished that one of us could accomplish what she was denied – to receive that degree, in person, on campus. I appreciate the opportunity to share this concern, as it symbolizes another of those experiences that really never go away, but hopefully, will help institute positive changes.

Thank you, and best wishes for continued success for the University of Arkansas.

Treopia G. Washington

January 6, 2011

Dear Ms. Washington:

I appreciate your taking the time to share your concern. Although I hate to hear of injustices like the one suffered by your mother, I appreciate the opportunity to show that the University of Arkansas is a very different institution today than it was in 1951.

We would very much like the opportunity to welcome you and your brothers to campus and to honor your mother and her tremendous accomplishment.

Would you please ask your brothers to share their thoughts regarding a fitting tribute? Considering the family has waited almost 60 years for this moment, I want to be certain that we do it "right."

Thanks again for writing, and best wishes for a wonderful 2011.

Sincerely,
G. David Gearhart
Chancellor
University of Arkansas

Our email correspondence evolved to a succession of telephone discussions with me, Ernest, and Dr. Charles Robinson, who was Vice Provost for Diversity at the university. In the final analysis, Chancellor Gearhart told me he would like to invite me and my son to the university, as guests of the university, to the May commencement ceremony to receive my mother's diploma.

Shortly after that, I was at the hair salon (again!) talking with one of the customers whose daughter had moved to Arkansas recently. I mentioned that I was going to Arkansas in a couple of weeks and told her about attending commencement to receive my mother's diploma. She said, "I must tell my daughter about this." I had no idea that her daughter was a writer for the AARP magazine. The next morning her daughter, whom I had never met, called me and said she told her editor about what was happening and her editor said, "We want that story."

May came and it was time to go to the university. We were registered at the hotel on the university campus. Prior to my arrival, two videographers from AARP were already there. When I registered at the front desk, the person said, "Oh, you're the person who's coming to get her mother's diploma!" Evidently the news had spread around the campus.

The first day after we arrived, we had a meeting with the chancellor in his office. When I went there, he was the most wonderful, warmest person. We talked and the videographers were there taking pictures all the time. The chancellor had three leatherbound diplomas made; one for each of us: myself, Ernest, and Scott. He also had done some research and found my mother's academic transcript, which he shared with us. Her transcript showed she had earned all A's and one B.

The next day the videographers asked me if they could come to my room to begin taping as I got ready. I said, "No, you wait in the lobby, and I will come down, and you can begin taping." When I met them in the lobby, they brought me to a walkway between a group of buildings. I didn't know but they had found that each class of graduates had their names inscribed in the year on that walkway. They had found my mother's name and wanted to show me. I had no idea before that it was there.

When I saw her name inscribed though, I saw that instead of her entire name, it just said "LS Green." The other names on the list included the full first and last name, but her name had been reduced to just her initials and last name. Given her experience with the graduation and the time period of the early 1950's, I felt that sort of fit the mold, taking away her individual identity. There were many attempts to erase people of color in different ways at that time.

We were escorted to a reception before the ceremony, May 14, 2011, and while we were there, one of the staff people came up and asked if I was Treopia Washington. He said, "Can you come with me for a minute? I just want to be sure that this photo is of your mother." So I identified the picture—it was her. I returned to the reception and then we were escorted into the arena. There were 20,000 people there for graduation. We were escorted to our seats in the first row marked "Family of Lothaire S. Green."

After we were seated, we were told that when the chancellor was ready to present the diploma, the marshals would come and bring us to the stage. Just before the graduate students were awarded their degrees, the Chancellor made a beautiful speech about my mother and how sixty years ago she was not allowed to come to graduation because of her color.

In part Chancellor Gearhart said in his speech, "As we all know the 1950s was a time in our nation's history when diversity and inclusion were not cherished principles by our society…during that time our university often failed to fully value and recognize the important achievements and contributions of African American students. This is a regrettable fact of our history. Today we have an opportunity to rectify a past injustice to one of our African American graduates. In 1951, just three years after the university had admitted its first African American student, Lothaire Scott Green completed the requirements for a master's degree in Education. She had every intention of taking part in the commencement ceremony to formally receive her degree but was advised by university officials not to attend. Lothaire Green's family is in attendance today. To them, we express our heartfelt respect and request they come to the stage to formally receive their mother's degree."

At that moment the marshals came to escort my son and me to the stage. The Chancellor presented me with her diploma, and the president of the university and the chairman of the board came forward to shake our hands. What I didn't realize was that while this was going on my mother's picture that I had identified earlier was being shown on the jumbotron. I'm glad I didn't see it because that may have overwhelmed me. It was enough to try to retain my composure as it was.

As soon as the ceremony was over, we were escorted off the stage and we walked down the center aisle. I remember a faculty member, who was White, rushed toward me in her cap and gown with tears in her eyes and she said, "I am so sorry that happened. I am so sorry," and she gave me a big hug. We walked back to our seats and the graduates were beginning to line up to process out of the arena, and one of the graduates said to me, "I am so happy that my graduation occurred on this day." It was unbelievable.

Shortly after, someone came and asked me to come over to where a local television news reporter wanted to interview me. I went over and talked to him for a few minutes. One of the questions the reporter asked me was something about if I realized this was going to be a historic moment. I said, "Well, you know when things happen, history isn't made until long after."

When it was all over, we returned to the hotel and stopped by the hotel lounge which was full of graduates and their families. I was talking with a waiter with whom I had made friends while I was staying there, and he brought me my glass of wine. Around 5:00 there was something on the television and I said, "I think there might be a news piece coming on that I might be in." Sure enough, that was the first story that came on the news. The people in the lounge turned around and told me how great they thought it was.

It's funny because I think if my mother were still alive, she would have said, "Treopia, you know you should not have done this." She instilled in us that you don't talk about yourself. She would say, "That's vain, that's ugly. It's unbecoming." But I think had I not written to the chancellor he would never have known that this had occurred. A wrong would have never been addressed.

Knowing we were football fans, the chancellor invited me and Todd back for a game to be guests in the skybox. He said, "You look at the schedule and you choose the game you want to come to." I chose the Auburn game. I remember growing up in Little Rock, the University of Arkansas would play Auburn, and it was big, big stuff, a big rivalry, but we could not go. So, I wanted to go to that game. And I did. Nobody else knew it, but for me, it was kind of an internal victory; significant because of history and the memory.

Several things happened after that. At the winter commencement that year Ernest was awarded an honorary doctorate. Following that I was invited and accepted membership on the Board of Advisors for the College of Education. While serving on the board at the first meeting I attended, I introduced myself and mentioned that my brother was one of the Little Rock Nine.

At the end of the meeting, the chair of the board came up to me and said, "I have got to tell you my husband was one of the Arkansas National Guardsman who was assigned to Little Rock Central High School, and he remembers your brother." She went on to tell me how impressed her husband had been by the way my brother carried himself. She and I became friends and would keep in touch in between board meetings.

About a year later Ernest was invited to a college in Jonesboro, Arkansas. I mentioned this to my friend, and she said she and her husband would be there too. So, they were able to meet Ernest and a picture was taken of Ernest with her husband and it appeared in the Little Rock newspaper.

All of these things that have happened in recent years, I think, are the fruition and outcomes of the things we were taught growing up. I have found through the years that if you approach people in the right way, they are open to seeing your point of view. If you do things the right way, you will more often than not achieve the results you want.

(L-R) Chancellor Gearhart, Treopia G. Washington, and Todd Washington, May 14, 2011 at the University of Arkansas spring commencement.

EPILOGUE

My father's service in World War I; my grandparents and parents' commitment to voting; my mother and aunt being part of the lawsuit for equal pay for Black teachers; Ernest being one of the first Black students to desegregate schools in America; my brother Scott being the first Black member of the Sheet Metalworkers Union Local 28 in New York City; and my contacting the University of Arkansas to let them know that my mother was denied commencement participation because of segregation—I see all of these things as connected. I see them as part of our commitment as American citizens and the work to bring into reality the words of our Constitution's Fourteenth Amendment that all would have equal protection under the law.

I think we are still trying to untangle the debacle created from the Jim Crow days and before.

When things are finally stabilized (which I don't think will happen in my lifetime), this will benefit everybody, not just the people who were disenfranchised, but *everybody*. The more we know about people whose lives are different than ours, the richer we will become. Developing future doctors, scientists, artists, astronauts— the list can go on and on. The realization and support of human potential benefits all of society. When people are not supported, and allowed to develop their talents and interests, we lose something of incalculable value. That's why the work for change, the fight, is not over. This effort must continue, to get closer to that ideal form of equity, equality, and fairness for citizens of color, to benefit all.

Civil rights and change take time, organization, and a lot of effort. Winning civil rights victories, and effectively overcoming past "wrongs," will depend on those who are willing to do things in a non-confrontational and nonviolent way, and through the court of law. This approach can be successful under our constitutional form of government. However, it takes much patience. A spirit of diplomacy has been my personal approach to situations where I would like to see change. I learned that from my mother. My family always stayed positive and used good judgement. Our mother and father led by example. This, I have tried to emulate in my life.

My Mother's Wisdom

My mother's wisdom has guided me throughout my life by internalizing her approach to dealing with life's problems. It really works. A clear understanding of what you can do helps to quell anxiety. The virtues she modeled—self-respect and respect for others—have always led me in the right direction. I hope in sharing her words, they can be of some guidance to others:

- Always do your best, whatever the task, because you never know what the next step will be.

- Follow your mind and do what is right.

- You're only as good as you are to other people. Helping people and being of service to others is what makes you a better person.

- In every situation in life, there are going to be people you like more than others and people who seem better to you than others—and that has nothing to do with race.

- Beauty is inner; it's how a person behaves that makes them beautiful.

- There should be no such thing as worry. If you have an issue, analyze it, decide what you can do about it and do what you can, and then leave it alone.

- There's no sense in losing a good night's sleep; there is nothing you can do about anything between 11:00 at night and 7:00 the next morning. You might as well have a good night's sleep, wake up the next day and deal with your issue then.

- Your job title does not define who you are.

- Remember, you can always do better...**In Spite Of.**

ACKNOWLEDGEMENTS

This book, *In Spite Of...*, would not be possible without the hard work, dedication, and understanding of my editor, Julia W. Monczunski Rutherford. Her commitment to this writing is beyond reproach. I can never thank her enough.

I am also forever grateful for the professional assistance from Paul Higbee, contributing editor at *South Dakota Magazine*, and copy editor, Julie Higbee Stiver. A special thank you to Sharla Steever and Dr. Scott Simpson for their invaluable contributions to this book.

A huge thank you to Traki Taylor, who, as Dean at Bowie State University, initiated this project. I will never forget her words, "Treopia, you have got to write a book."

Finally, my appreciation to all who have endured bits and pieces of this book, and have provided support, and helpful commentary.

Made in United States
Orlando, FL
03 April 2023

31696595R00095